BURN

Melting into the Image of Jesus

Eric William Gilmour

Sonship
International

BURN
Melting into the Image of Jesus
by Eric William Gilmour
Sonship International, Inc.

E-MAIL: ERIC@SONSHIP-INTERNATIONAL.ORG
WEBSITE: SONSHIP-INTERNATIONAL.ORG
TWITTER/@SONSHIPINTL
FACEBOOK/ERICGILMOUR

Printed in the United States of America
ISBN-13: 978-1727530940
ISBN-10: 1727530942

Scripture quotations taken from the New American Standard Bible®. Copyright © 1960, 1962, 1963, 1968, 1971, 1972, 1973, 1975, 1977, 1995 by The Lockman Foundation Used by permission. (www.Lockman.org)

Cover Design by Daniel Mironichenko
Copyright © 2012 Wondrous Design
www.wondrousdesigns.com

Editing and Typesetting by Kathy Curtis
Christian Book Production Services
www.christianbookformat.com

"Seeking oneness with God through surrender; raising up the Jesus people."

DEDICATION

I dedicate this book to all the melted men not content to sit near the Fire, but were fiercely fixed on thrusting themselves into Him Who is Fire, both those who continue to labor today and those whose voices speak from the grave. I am forever indebted to you, for your hearts' union with God revealed the transcendence of His life to me. I love you and thank God for your lives, and I thank you for allowing God to take you up into Himself. I also dedicate this book as a call for all believers everywhere to let God burn you away so that only He remains.

ENDORSEMENTS

"This book is a genuine call to the Church to return to the roots of Christianity, namely, love for Jesus Christ. Take it, read it, and allow it to take you back to Jesus."

~Evangelist Daniel Kolenda
(CEO and President of Christ for all Nations)

"I am convinced within the depths of my heart that life's greatest achievement is to genuinely burn with a love for Jesus. It is the all in all. Jesus is life and life is Jesus. I believe Eric loves the Master. May the flames in this book be used to melt you into a holy union with Love Himself."

~Evangelist Michael Koulianos
(Founder of Jesus Image)

"Many people talk about the Fire of God. Yet, a man or woman who really burns with this Fire always leaves a trail of changed lives, miracles, and the tangible presence of Jesus. I have met very few burning with this type of Holy Spirit Fire. Eric Gilmour is one of these burning men. Be aware as you read these pages. Fire may grab ahold of you. Come, Holy Spirit."

~Russell Benson
*(Executive Administrator of Christ for all Nations,
the ministry of Reinhard Bonnke and Daniel Kolenda)*

"In a day of superficialism and false surrender, there is a call in this book for authenticity. Many claim to be anointed of God or full of the Spirit of God, but so few of these do anything for God. There is a trumpet blast from heaven still blowing with the words: 'Go! Multitudes are on their way to a Christ-less Eternity.'"

~Greg Gordon
*(Founder of the largest internet revival resource center
in the world, www.sermonindex.com)*

"For many years, I have feasted on quotes and short compilations from other authors, those piercing arrows of truth that cut to the heart of the matter and, in a few words, do what lengthy volumes cannot do. Eric Gilmour has a gift for compiling such penetrating truths, and his new book will help fuel a deeper, holy fire in your heart. Read and be ignited!"

~Dr. Michael L. Brown
(President, FIRE School of Ministry, Concord, NC)

"*BURN* doesn't fall in the category of just another Christian book. It is a series of essays in which the present world chaos is described; the need for Christians who are all out for Christ and the price they have to pay. The promises of God are immense and this booklet only teaches one theology: '*Christ is perfect theology.*' Don't miss the book. You will read it more than once."

~Roel Velema
(Netherlands Minister Founder of Christ, The Church and the Coming Kingdom)

"This book burns and will ignite a cold heart and a weak Church. The fire is real, the zeal contagious, and the wisdom trustworthy to call us into the depths of Jesus Christ."

~Dr. Robert Gladstone
(Pastor of Kings People Church in North Carolina)

"In a Church-age of differing measures, where the saints often feel compelled to choose one truth or manifestation over another, Eric brings us back to the central issue out of which all else flows. This book, penned by a man burning with the Spirit, acts as a Burning guide, taking both young and old, novice and leader, into the depths of the experience of Jesus Christ."

~David Popovici
(Founder of Kingdom Gospel Mission)

INTRODUCTION

God is raising up the Jesus people. It is His eternal desire to multiply the perfect wisdom, life, and power of His Son. It is burning inside of His heart to possess His people. God possession is the formula to create the Jesus people. There is only one route to God possession: God obsession. The Jesus people are the God-cravers, not intimidated by man or intimidators of man. The Jesus people are tender, pure, and non-judgmental, all the while speaking the truth dripping with gentle love. The Jesus people have lost all other interests and cling to Christ in absolute dependency. The Jesus people are radiant with humility, broken by His presence, and aflame with living-loving surges of power that exercises the dominion of Jesus in the earth. The Jesus people are bought by His blood and possessed by His Spirit. I write this book to stir you, to equip you, and to bring you into the experience of God Himself and addiction to His divine sweetness. The reconciliation is the restoration of God and man finding pleasure in each other. Holiness is the fruit of being addicted to the maximum pleasure of life, which is God Himself. When God pleases us and we please God, therein is the practice of love and eternal life. I write this book to fuel the revolution of the Jesus people. May it be a manual to you and to the generations to come, erecting the pillars of the Jesus people. Each chapter is chosen specifically to cover the most important facets of the life that seeks to be possessed by God. It is of utmost necessity that we are the well-rounded full expression of Jesus, and not partial. To focus on part rather than the whole is to set ourselves up for a failure. We want Him in His fullness. So rise up, mystical wonder workers who seek oneness with God through surrender, and demonstrate the power of the Spirit in character, charisma, and wisdom. Be set on fire with the substance of God! Fire is not fervency, but no vacancy. Fire is not prayer volume or evangelistic busyness; it is, rather, being eaten up by the substance of God till nothing is left but bridal union and oneness. Total consumption is what we want. How many will join me in a simple prayer? God, I surrender all. Light me ablaze with Yourself and may Your substance in and on my life cause me to be a light to the world. BURN ME AWAY!

TABLE OF CONTENTS

———～∾∽～———

"Are the things you're living for worth Christ dying for?"
~Leonard Ravenhill

"Don't ever slow down going after God."
~Stephen L. Hill

"You want to know what your ministry is? BURN,
wherever you are. That is your ministry."
~Robert Gladstone

"One of these days we will get sick and tired of the spiritual
bankruptcy that we live in and the joke that our lives often
are and we will get serious with God."
~Dr. Michael L. Brown

"Beloved, for the sake of a lost and dying world, pay any
price, get God's power, and set the prisoners free."
~John G. Lake

"God has nothing less for us than to be flames!"
~Smith Wigglesworth

———～∾∽～———

CHAPTER 1

BURNING FOR JESUS

"They loved not their lives unto death...." ~Revelation 12:11

W hat is it about that rare kind of Christian who, in the core of his being, burns with the desire to impact his generation with the power of the Holy Spirit, leave a legacy that will stir others to do the same, and haunt the complacent till they breathe their last breath? Knowing he has genuinely been issued a divine call, he chooses to live it, breathe it, and empty every ounce of his life upon that which he has directed his heart toward, namely, God and His Gospel.

What happened to this Christian to cause him to exchange his natural desire to govern his own path, create his own reputation, and live in the common self-preservation current of life, for a courageous, relentless zeal that drives him to seek God with all his heart and pour his life out on Jesus? How did he come to reduce his life to maintain a steady, simple, uncompromising and continual pursuit of God, and men?

"Wisdom is not collected truths shut up in books to be read, but demonstrated by blood sunk into the soil of the earth; dripping from a God-indwelt ripped flesh nailed to a cross."

I submit to you, that this man has seen the cross. As Charles Spurgeon said, *"Any life that is not bowed down beneath the cross has yet to see it."*[1] The wisdom of God is an octave too high for the minds of men. Such heavenly wisdom is not wisdom that can be explained; it must be demonstrated. The blood of our mangled, humiliated, despised, and rejected God alone can display such glorious wisdom.

Wisdom is not learned truths shut up in books to be read, but demonstrated by blood sunk into the soil of the earth; dripping from a God-indwelt ripped flesh nailed to a cross.

There exists an inseparable link between such a revelation of the cross and such an eternally significant life. This eternally significant life has been gripped by the humility and selfless love of the God-man who gives Himself to be painfully punished to save those who deserve to be punished. He has been filled with the same selfless love (through the Holy Spirit) that causes a man to respond to God's emptied life, with the emptying of his own life, so that he may be continually filled and consistently overflowing with God alone. He has had that *dying love* of God poured out in his heart by the Holy Ghost (Romans 5:5). The most pure and sure evidence of the *filling* of the Holy Spirit is nothing other than having our eyes opened to see a crucified Christ, as God's wisdom, producing an inward wellspring of love for Jesus. The evidence of the Holy Spirit resting upon our lives is none other than supernatural power. As Bill Johnson says, *"He is in me for my sake and He is upon me for yours."*[2] He dwells inside for character and outside for power, only in the life that is wholly His.

SPIRIT-DOMINATED LIFE

Why do you think that such a Spirit-immersed life is so attractive, so inspiring, and so challenging? Is it not because all of us Christians have tucked away inside of ourselves a desire for such a God possession no matter how hidden, yet no less real? Is it not that we desire to live wholeheartedly in love with Him, so intensely immersed in Him, and so deeply aware of Him that in our last moments of life we know deep inside that we, through surrender, have invested sincerely, truthfully, and wholeheartedly in the only One worthy to live and die for? Is this not the spirituality of the glorious Christian martyr, looked on at the time of his death as a fool, but honored in the future as a man who has chosen not to suppress that violent Jesus obsession that every Christian has inside by the Holy Spirit?[3]

I believe that the most Spirit-dominated men are those whose lives are lost in the abyss of absolute surrender to God! God swallows up the natural life of such a man, who has chosen not to suppress that Spirit installation of absolute abandonment. He is absorbed in His God, dominated internally and consequently free from any fear that is fueled by self-preservation. Can you see the connection that resembles Jesus' life? The God-absorbed man is a martyr even while he lives. His life is burned away by the life of God.

"I believe that the most Spirit-dominated men are those whose lives are lost in the abyss of absolute surrender to God!"

At the end of Leonard Ravenhill's life he was asked the age-old question, *"If you could go back and do it all again, would you do anything different?"* His answer was the best I ever heard. He replied, *"No, I spent all the time with Him that I could."*[4]

"The proof of our love for God is not in how much time we spend in meetings or chasing drug addicts or whatever. But in how much time we spend with Him. How much time do we spend listening to God?" (Leonard Ravenhill)[5]

A life lived looking unto Jesus will receive the divine fire to burn away every obstruction and shine the living light of the Godhead into the earth!

WILL YOU BE DOMINATED?

Here I am, and you as well, with the opportunity before us to choose to continue to be haunted by the lives of those who gave themselves wholly unto Jesus, or to choose as they have, to give both our life and time to the only One worth the liquid soul in our veins. Every man will one day have his final thoughts; he will turn around on life's path and see where his blood has been spent. There, in that moment, will undoubtedly be the true test of a man's love. For our lives are one long love letter to God, written today and presented to Him and read aloud before all saints of the ages and angels in glory, tomorrow.

God's desire for us is to have an unquenchable love for Jesus that results in a transformation into His likeness. As He flows into us with His life and light, our life is poured out for the world. Christianity is not about living our lives, but giving our lives. The love, with which God loved us, is the same love with which we love Him and others.[6]

We all only have one earthly life. One fragile life made up of time, consisting of moments, and even as you read this now, your life heads toward its end.

So, as the martyr smiles at the ax, for in its shine he sees Christ's costly legacy, the coward weeps at his past, for in his tears he sees his own lethargy. He remembers his complacency, his decadency, and sees his weak, lost life, blown away in the wind, eternally worthless and insignificant. Though many people don't like to talk about this anymore, compromised Christians get nothing (Jeremiah 29:13). God wants all of your heart, because He deserves all your heart. And, He has the right to demand it, simply because He knows that no one else loves you like He does, nor can any fulfill your soul like He can.

TOLERATION

I submit to you that most American Christians are killed by toleration. We are destroyed by what we tolerate. Our idolatry is in our toleration that creates an admixture of adultery and a love affair with some lesser lover. Toleration leaves the door behind you, unlocked. Toleration is that drop of poison in the glass of purified water. Toleration is compromise. But, a burning attraction to the Son of God will light the oil of the Spirit on a man's life and make him, and consequently his life, a lamp that burns brightly (John 5:35). It will seal him off from the enemy. Loving Jesus with all of our hearts is the universal solution. Being in love with Jesus is the end of toleration. God is not asking us to love Him the most. He is asking us to love Him only. Many people say that they "love Jesus." But our downfall is that we don't love Him alone. It was Basilea Schlink who wrote, *"To love Jesus with all my heart means I must let go of all other loves."*[7]

WHY WRITE SUCH THOUGHTS?

To what end or conclusion are such sobering thoughts? I pray these words will resound with an everlasting echo that walks by our side, speaking into our ears on a crowded street, and also sits with us when we are alone, in order to haunt us in the silence of solitude.

Are you in love with Jesus alone? Loving Jesus is the only preparation for the day of accountability that plunges deep enough to grip the root of the Adamic life.[8]

Meditate on these passages.

2 Corinthians 5:9-11 "Therefore also we have as our ambition...to be pleasing to Him. *For we must all appear before the judgment seat of Christ*, that each one may be recompensed for his *works in the body*, according to what he has done, whether good or bad. Therefore knowing the fear of the Lord, we persuade men."

1 Peter 1:17 "And if you address as Father the One who *impartially judges according to each man's work*, conduct yourselves in fear during the time of your stay *upon earth.*"

Romans 14:12 "So then each one of us shall *give account of himself* to God."

Matthew 16:24-27 "Then Jesus said to His disciples, "*If anyone wishes to come after Me, let him deny himself*, and take up his cross, and follow Me. "*For whoever wishes to save his life shall lose it*; but whoever loses his life for My sake shall find it. "For what will a man be profited, if he gains the whole world, and forfeits his soul? Or what will a man give in exchange for his soul? "For the Son of Man is going to come in the glory of His Father with His angels; and will then *recompense every man according to his works."*

Romans 8:29 "He predestined us to be conformed to the *image of His Son."*

HIS IMAGE IS OUR WORKS

Notice that the word *"work"* and *"works"* are connected with recompenses; exact payment for services rendered. It is not by self-efforts, but by surrender to the abiding Father within that these works are wrought. Jesus said, *"My Father who abides in Me, does His works."* There are good works that were created to walk out in Christ (Ephesians 2:10). But the error rises when we fail to see the definition of *"good"* as God defines it. The first mention of the word *"good"* in Scripture is in Genesis chapter 1. God created it and, *"it was good."* The word *"good"* is pointing to the fact that these works of God have their origin in the only One Who is good. Jesus told us that there is none good, but the Father (Luke 18:19). Also Scripture states, *"...every good...gift comes down from the...Father"* (James 1:17). Notice the glory goes to the Father when others see our *"good works"* (Matthew 5:16). Also notice Jesus' words, *"...many good works have I shown you from My Father"* (John 10:32). Again, note that the origin of these good things is God. The *"good works"* that are entrusted to us to perform while on the earth are none other than things wrought out of a yielded life. We are to be conduits: *"A channel for conveying water...."*[9] *"The*

only thing that pleases God is what He does Himself."[10]
*"The amazing thing about grace, is that the Father is going
to reward us for the things that He pulled off."*[11] There is
nothing like Jesus in whom our God comes to die for
us, so that He might live in us and work through us,
only to later reward us for it.

I remember a story that changed my view of the judgment seat of Christ forever. A dear preacher woke
up in the middle of the night in a cold sweat, having
had a dream in which he saw the judgment seat. As
he drew near to the throne, and closer to his moment
of accountability, he began to rehearse in his mind the
things that he had accomplished for God while on
the earth and prepared the tip of his tongue with his
résumé' of service.

Just before he was able to release such a self-applica-
tion before God, God said to him, *"Come closer. I want
to see how much of my Son I can see inside of you."*[12]

It is not about how much we can do for God, but rather,
God for us on the cross, God in us by the Spirit, God
out of us as His works, and God's reward to us at the
Judgment! No other quality of works will survive the
test of fire (1 Corinthians 3; Romans 11:36).

THE CALL TO SONSHIP

I issue a challenge to you, as I often do to myself, in
light of such a coming day: fearfully conduct yourself as a Christian heading toward an impartial day of

judgment by living a yielded life, free from the obstructions of self.

The Judgment Day will not be a day to take a written exam to test your knowledge, nor a day to look over your résumé' of service, but a day in which God will contrast your image with the image of His Son (Romans 8:29).

There is only one life to offer up to Him who gave His life for us. As we consistently lay that life down upon the altar, He will burn it up. His fire will touch every aspect of our being. Is He dominating you?

Take a serious look at your…

Mind (thought life)
Motives (the why behind your actions)
Mouth (the idle words/preaching)
Money (stewardship of substance)
Ministry (what God is doing through you)
Message (what you are teaching)
Marriage (what your spouse has to say about you)
Minutes (how you spend your time)

THE EMPOWERMENT

If I know anything at all in my spirit, I know this: we look like Jesus in exact proportion to our love for Him. Nothing will so take over our soul and conform it to the image of Jesus as when our souls are set gazing upon Him. Following Jesus is setting your life gaze upon Him and then adjusting whatever you must adjust to keep that gaze upon Him as He progresses forward as leader. This is what is meant by the call, *"Follow Me"* (John 10:27).

Kathryn Kuhlman said, *"Holiness is being led by the Spirit."*[13] One of the clearest things God has ever said to me was while I was riding in the back seat of a car to a hotel in Germany in 2010. He said, *"Holiness is the fruit of being addicted to the maximum pleasure of life, which is God Himself."* The Christian who is most separated unto God is the man who is most satisfied with his God, and the Christian who is most worldly is that Christian who is least satisfied with his God. To live a complacent Christian life is to testify to the world that God is not enough. The most confident life before God at the judgment seat of Christ in heaven is a life that was lived gazing upon Jesus on earth.

CONCLUSION

I grew up in the Church my entire life, and I never heard a message that stuck the razor blade of God into my soul until I saw Steve Hill, anointed with the Holy Spirit and fearlessly piercing men with the arrows of holy

"He predestined us to be conformed to the image of His Son."

conviction. I met Jesus the first day that I saw Steve Hill. I can't tell you the amount of times I have watched love for Jesus burst out in tears and fall from Steve Hill's face. For this reason I feel so strongly about a life totally laid down at the altar; for the compromised, complacent, cold minister is the alibi of the lukewarm.

I write this book to lay before you a call to fall back in love with Jesus today; a call to go after Him like never before; a call to be immersed in the Holy Spirit. What does that mean? It means spending as much time with Him as you can. *"To be much for God, we must be much alone with God"* (Leonard Ravenhill).

I have been privileged to see men ablaze with God. I can still hear the gut-wrenching call from Dr. Michael L. Brown in 1999, *"Some of us want to sit back and relax, but now is not the time to sit back and coast. Now is the time to press in! Now is the time where it either breaks for the glory of God or we lose all hope for revival. Now is the time where we either seize the moment, or look back with everlasting shame that we missed it."*[14]

There is only one time period in which it is designated for us to learn obedience and choose to lay down our lives in response to His life laid down for us. We must redeem the time (Ephesians 5:16) because the days are evil. God can forgive you, but time will never forgive you. Time is a grace more valuable than anything, for no amount of riches can redeem it. Wherever you are, whoever you are, surrender everything and go into God that He might come out of you. There is simply no other way to resemble His Son and find confidence at the day of His appearing!

"...abide in Him that when He appears we may have confidence and not be ashamed before Him at His coming"
(1 John 2:28).

Throughout this book we will look into the ascent of the soul into the state of unbroken awareness of His abiding presence and its effects.

—∽—

"The knowledge of our own poverty is what brings us to the proper place where Jesus accomplishes His work."
~Oswald Chambers

"We make humility the chief thing when we admire Him." ~Andrew Murray

"Simplicity is loving intent upon Him alone, seeking no other person or thing." ~John Wesley

"Humility says, 'I am nothing and I have nothing.'"
~Walter Hilton

"God said: 'The higher they are in heaven, the more humble they are in themselves, and the closer to Me — the more in love with Me.'" ~Brother Lawrence

"You cannot expect anything from God unless you put yourself in the right place, that is, a beggar at His footstool. Then He will hear you, and not until then."
~Charles Spurgeon

—∽—

CHAPTER 2

BURNING AWAY

"Blessed are the poor in spirit...
...for theirs is the Kingdom." ~Matthew 5:3

"Nothing in my hands I bring, simply to the cross
I cling."[15]

Turning in the core of my heart is a fire, not a fire for "power" or "passion," but for the restoration of internal poverty in the Christian life. I extend to you the case of internal poverty, without which a man is locked away in the cell of self. He is chained in the irons of worth. He is fixed progressing in the wrong direction. As Dietrich Bonhoeffer said, *"If you board the wrong train, it makes no sense to sprint down the corridor in the right direction."*[16] Or, what does it matter if we climb to the top of the mountain and realize that we climbed the wrong mountain? Without humility, all efforts are worthless. Internal poverty is the dethroning of self that clears the throne of our lives for the King to have His rightful place. Have you wondered why the Kingdom is given to the poor? The rule of God, the King's domain, and the power of Kingdom life are ignited by poverty alone. The spiritual man is bound to internal poverty; he has fastened himself to poverty by his own will, having learned its attractiveness to God. He is gripped by the total freedom of bondage to Jesus Christ. Without internal poverty a man rejects such binding, attractiveness, and consequently forfeits true liberty.

THE VALUE OF POVERTY

"The rule of God, the King's domain, and the power of Kingdom life are ignited by poverty alone."

Poverty is greater than power. A man may possess miracles and healing, yet be disconnected from the disposition that draws God's heart to him: *"I am poor and needy"* (Psalm 86:1; 40:17; 70:5; 109:22). The poor man understands that he doesn't have what he most severely needs, and without aid from the outside he will most definitely perish. Are you as poor today as that day you first called upon His name to save you from your sins?

Poverty is greater than prayer. A man may pray hours upon hours and yet possess not that quality that bestows grace on his being. *"God resists the proud but gives grace to the humble"* (James 4:6; 1 Peter 5:5). Once, two men came to the same place to pray. Oh, how two individuals can perform the same actions from widely different motives! One man came to boast of his right living and the other came to cry out for mercy (Luke 18:13). God alone sees the heart and the heart alone sees God (1 Samuel 16:7; Proverbs 16:2) and internal poverty is His delight.

Poverty is greater than passion. A man may impress many in the assembly with volume and fervor, yet be inwardly bankrupt, because he finds great value in himself. This man is far removed from the riches of the Kingdom being bestowed in his soul through poverty alone, for the Kingdom is the possession of the poor. Francis de Sales said, *"Nothing can so effectually humble us as the consideration of what He has done for us and what we have done against Him."*[17] Oh brothers, poverty is that for which there exists no substitute.

Poverty is that ingredient without which there exists no potential for rise in God. Poverty is the daily and constant reaching for mercy by revelation of our inability and nothingness without His presence. Poverty is united with dependency. We will never be exempt from poverty's dependency. As David Ravenhill said, *"We never graduate from dependency."*[18]

> **"Poverty is that ingredient without which there exists no potential for rise in God."**

ATTRACTIVE TRINITY

"Poverty is the recognition of our wicked state without God's presence, which thrusts us into dependency on His presence and manifests itself in humble hearts and lives."

Lust we for GLORY? *"That faculty of the soul that pants for glory is implanted of God"* (R. Govet).[19] Have you an inward burning attraction to be absorbed up into your God? *Poverty* is the only route, *dependency* the only way, and *humility* the only foundation. For this trinity, there exists no substitute.

Poverty is the recognition of our wicked state without God's presence, which thrusts us into dependency on His presence and manifests itself in humble hearts and lives.

David Popovici said to me on the phone the other day, *"The day we wake up without a casting of ourselves upon His mercy, we are finished."* I would add, the *moment* that we cease to cast ourselves upon His mercy we are finished. Temptation is a reminder of what we are apart from His presence in our lives. How many times have we all failed in some way and disappointed ourselves and God? After fourteen years of following Jesus, I see now more than ever, that every failure in my life was first a failure to depend upon Him. Sins are just the fruit of the root sin, which is, independence. The absolute formula for destruction is to stop clinging to God (Psalm 16:8; 32:8; 53:8). The issue is attachment or detachment.

As the rain rests upon the ground after the storm, it yearns to return back to the high place from which it has fallen. It can only long for such a return, till the sunrays shine down upon its humble state, causing it to rise again through evaporation into its desired residence. So, we as men have fallen from a height of glory. *"For all...fall short of the glory of God"* (Romans 3:23). We all, as redeemed men, long to live in the heights from which we have fallen. Man is burning internally for glory to be restored.

"...every failure in my life was first a failure to depend upon Him."

I submit to you today, that without internal poverty, that causes us to rest upon the ground and look to the rays of the Son, there is no identification with the positional restored glory now and no promise of its fullness in the age to come. And most certainly, there is no connection with its transforming reality in our daily life; for Christ's humble dying must be plugged into the humbled sinner to ever produce a humble life.

POVERTY VS. INTELLECTUALITY

Cerebral arguments and superstar-superhero preaching all stem from a lack of poverty. Poverty alone ensures the glory to God. A value in us robs Him of the glory that He deserves. He takes the beggar from the dunghill (Psalm 113:7) — not the prince from the palace or the theologian from the seminary.

33

All we see as holy acts and ways in men are empty without poverty as its heartbeat. A humble heart is the wisest heart. Andrew Murray wrote, *"Humility is the pathway unto death."*[20] For what amount of heavenly knowledge or sage-like wisdom gained through many years could ever compare to a demonstration of lowliness chosen by God to save men? God was desperately trying to communicate to us what wisdom truly is. Wisdom is not retained information or even spiritual insights, but rather a broken heart that breaks its pride to lay down a broken body to fix a broken people.

> *"Let this mind be in you, which was also in Christ Jesus: Who, being in the form of God, thought it not robbery to be equal with God:* **But made himself of no reputation, and took upon him the form of a servant,** *and was* **made in the likeness of men:** *And being found in fashion as a man,* **he humbled himself,** *and* **became obedient unto death,** *even the death of the cross. Wherefore God also hath highly exalted him, and given him a name which is above every name...."*
> ~Philippians 2:5-9

I am well aware of the fact that I, as one man, do not possess a full picture of God, and my heart is longing for the Church to take her fullness again. And, though there are many camps that have different emphases in God, in receiving as much as I can from each camp, I believe that arrogance is heightened when a man claims now that which God has set for the future. There is no fullness now. There exists no sinless perfection now. There is no full seeing now; just as much as there exists no reigning King Jesus in Jerusalem now. And, anyone who wishes to preach "fullness now" or boasts in their intellectualism, is missing the

> *"...anyone who wishes to preach 'fullness now' or boasts in their intellectualism, is missing the heart of wisdom Himself, namely poverty, humility, and brokenness."*

heart of wisdom Himself, namely poverty, humility, and brokenness. Anyone finding the slightest satisfaction or interest in the failures and judgment of others knows nothing of poverty, dependency, and humility, for the value of themselves has blinded them to the nakedness of their own soul.

We do not possess independently anything of value, and that which we do possess in Him is a deposit of a fullness to come (2 Corinthians 1:22; 5:5; Ephesians 1:14). And, that which is possessed is penetrated into us by humility alone. *"Beloved, if you have ever seen yourself, you will know that you are never going to be anything other than what you were"* (Paris Reidhead).[21] Paul the apostle, who was closer than anyone alive today to a fullness of the image of Christ, released in a human life said, *"...as for me and my flesh, there is no good thing"* (Romans 7). He understood His nothingness as God's power; seeing strength perfected in weakness (2 Corinthians 12:9); seeing a treasure in an earthen vessel, so that the greatness of God's power would be of Himself and not from ourselves (2 Corinthians 4).

Such thoughts are in no way an advocating of sin, but rather, the way to true holiness of heart. Poverty blesses man with the riches of God's grace that makes a man truly holy from the inside out; for it is in the poor soul alone that the Holy Spirit finds a resting place. Otherwise man is occupying the whole of the throne himself. God finds no room in a man full of himself. In simple terms, a man FULL of the Holy Spirit has no room for anything else.

"All we see as holy acts and ways in men are empty without poverty as its heartbeat."

Listen, I fear that educated Christians in America like us will educate ourselves out of poverty and into a delusion of "fullness now," intellectual know-it-all-ness, and deceive ourselves into a mind-set that is far from the current divine situation concerning God, man, mercy, power, and redemption. Our power is not found in the cerebral realm. It is found in death. It is not found in a new vision of ourselves or in a puffed up identity that changes the way we carry ourselves; it is found in His mercy. It is His mercy that works every day in us; His mercy that quickens us back to life from the death of truly understanding that we cannot ever in our own selves please Him or move toward Him. If we know anything, let it be our continual sins forgiven and our personal poverty coming face-to-face with His boundless love and His timeless mercy, restoring and keeping us in the power of His presence.

POVERTY AND PRESENCE

In 1 Thessalonians chapter 1, Paul is thanking God for the Church's *"labor of love, works of faith and stead-fastness of hope…in the presence of God."* The presence of God is the ground for faith that works, love that labors, and hope that is steadfast. I can't help but see it as a scene from an old UFO movie where the powerful UFO activates and charges all the power tools, lights, cars, and everything electric as it flies over the old farmer's house in the middle of Nebraska fields. That is the

"Dependency sustains the Kingdom's rule in which a humble character is the inevitable product."

activation of the presence of God. As He draws near, our love, which was otherwise frozen, comes alive; our faith, which was otherwise dead, is working; and our hope, which was otherwise forgotten, is realized. Internal poverty is the landing pad for the Kingdom, which is to say, the King. Dependency sustains the Kingdom's rule in which a humble character is the inevitable product. And such a way to such a presence is the activation of a Christ-like life. Poverty gives the Kingdom, humility receives exaltation, and dependency bears forth fruit, which glorifies the Father.

THE MARY MIXTURE

What could possibly be greater in the world than being overshadowed by God's Holy Spirit to birth the Christ into the world? God not only chose Mary because her lineage went back to David (2 Samuel 7:14), but also because of the mixture of four qualities that I believe are highly flammable to the Holy Spirit. I believe that these three qualities are the essence of what God sees as a landing pad for His Glory. Remember, wherever God lets His Glory rest, it is there that Jesus is made manifest.

All of God's desires can be summed up in a revelation of Jesus. Everything that God does is to reveal Jesus. Any work that you have before you to accomplish in God is to reveal Jesus. This will not be possible apart from His manifest presence. It is never possible to truly see Jesus without the presence and work of the Holy Spirit.

"Poverty gives the Kingdom, humility receives exaltation, and dependency bears forth fruit, which glorifies the Father."

The first thing that must be noted about Mary is that she was a *"virgin"* (Luke 1:34). Virginity is typical of *"purity."* It is to not have had relations with another outside of covenant. Mary's virginity is symbolic of being unspotted by the world (James 1:27). It is to have not had any intercourse or transaction with this world. It is to be separated and consecrated unto One. Madame Guyon said, *"True simplicity regards Jesus alone."*[22] Such simplicity is what Paul was jealous for in 2 Corinthians 11:2-3, *"For I am jealous*

over you with a godly jealousy: for I espoused you to one hus-
*band, that I might **present you as a pure virgin** to Christ.*
But I fear, lest by any means, as the serpent beguiled Eve in
his craftiness, your minds should be corrupted from the sim-
plicity and the purity that is toward Christ."

The second thing that must be noted about Mary is her
humility (Luke 1:48). When the angel came to her and
told her what she was to do, her response was amazing.
"How can this be, for I am a virgin?" She recognized her
inability. She recognized her absolute state of powerlessness to perform the deed herself. Her humility was
revealed in the surrender of presenting her bankruptcy
at the feet of His riches.

The third thing that must be noted about Mary is the
fact that she was a *"bondslave"* (Luke 1:48). A bondslave is a slave "by will," meaning, if a slave was
released and he made a choice to remain a slave to his
owner, though he was freed, he was then considered
a bondslave. Mary was the Lord's. Her existence was
completely His. God saw this heart inside of her and
He knew He could rest upon her.

The fourth is the fact that Mary *"feared the Lord"* (Luke
1:50). Humility and the fear of the Lord are united
(Proverbs 22:4). Without the anchor of the fear of the
Lord, we will float off into airy places where there exists
no ground of reality. God said to me, *"If you remove the*
fear of the Lord, you will create an emasculated Christianity
that cannot overcome the evil one." The fear of the Lord is
the irreplaceable foundation for wisdom (Proverbs 1:7).

"God must overshadow us with the Holy Ghost to birth His purpose in the earth, which is namely, revealing His Son Jesus." The summary is this: God must overshadow us with the Holy Ghost to birth His purpose in the earth, which is namely, revealing His Son Jesus. There is no other way, for we need God's power to do God's work. His work is in a realm that is higher than that which we are acquainted with. If the poverty of humility is mixed with the fear of the Lord, the purity of virginity, and the loving not our lives, in slavery unto God by our own will, there is nothing that is more flammable to the fire of the Holy Spirit in the earth.

Those of you who desire to break into God like few have, ask yourself:

- Where am I impure?
- Where have I lacked the fear of God?
- Where do I need the blood of Jesus to wash me, fresh?
- Where have I lifted myself up?
- Have I failed to fall on my face and acknowledge my bankruptcy?
- Where have I loved my own life?
- Where have I not laid my life down before the Lord?
- Am I freshly filled with the Holy Ghost?
- Am I living continually being filled with the Holy Spirit?

This mixture is the Mary mixture. It births the divine things in the earth. It births a wonderful revelation of Jesus. Our model is the Son of God. He is only made manifest in us as much as we can host Him in our lives through such a real, absolute surrender, utter dependency, and total reliance.

THE SECRET

"Preserve me, O God: for in Thee do I put my trust."
~Psalm 16:1

The word *"preserve"* has to do with *"keeping something in its original state."* The fact that David is reaching out for another to preserve him implies that he recognizes that he cannot preserve himself. Our original state in God is purity, holy and undefiled from this world. God has taken us out of the mud and washed us as squeaky clean as His very own Son, by the blood of His very own Son. David is acknowledging his inability and helplessness to stay clean, remain undefiled, or be preserved in purity. The psalmist often cried, *"Save me"* (Psalm 3:7; 6:4; 7:1; 22:21; 31:2). But this cry is different. It is not a cry to be rescued; it is a cry to remain in the rescued state—not to be made pure, but to remain pure.

I extend to you the God-revealed route to a sustained purity and preserving in God, *"...for in Thee do I put my trust."* All victory begins with this heart, *"I can't do it!"* When man reaches the end of himself, there and nowhere else does he find the beginning of God. Our hearts must cry, *"I cannot preserve myself, so I look to You."*

Jesus, talking of the salvation that is impossible with men and only possible with God (Matthew 19:26), made a parallel with the serpent lifted up in the Old Testament (John 3:14; Numbers 21:9). The only path of salvation from the snake poison in the body of the Israelites was to lift their eyes to the golden serpent to be healed. So, when a man simply looks in surrender to Jesus, not only once to be saved, but consistently to be preserved, he finds his glorious rescue and union with God (John 15:5).

None of us did anything to attain our salvation (Ephesians 2:8,9). We simply recognized that we could not save ourselves and we cried from a dark pit, the helpless cry of a condemned sinner, *"God, save me!"* God in His mercy reached down and saved us from such a state and doom (John 3:16-17; Romans 8:1; Ephesians 2:1-2). God is not waiting for you to reach a certain point of desperation before He rushes in to preserve or save; He is waiting for you to empty your inward poison by looking away from yourself and unto Him.

"He is waiting for you to empty your inward poison by looking away from yourself and unto Him."

It is not that He refuses to come to man until…but that man will not respond to His having already come to us. Jesus simply summed up all of Christianity in one phrase, *"Come to Me..."* (Matthew 11:28). That isn't when He saves you; that coming to Him IS your saving.

I submit to you today, that the same utter dependency, total reliance, and absolute surrender to God that your soul reached to God with to be born again, is the same cry that must be lived in for the sustained victorious spiritual life. That is the secret. That is the most mature perspective in God that there is. I CANNOT DO IT! I need You, Oh, I need You; every hour, I need You.

> *"I submit to you today, that the same utter dependency, total reliance, and absolute surrender to God that your soul reached to God with to be born again, is the same cry that must be lived in for the sustained victorious spiritual life."*

Jesus said, *"The Son can do nothing of Himself; I do nothing on My own initiative"* (John 5:19; 8:28). Oh struggling brother, tired Christian, and weak-willed, complacent, distant follower of Christ, you cannot maintain yourself. As long as you try to maintain yourself, you are already in failure, for no amount of Adamic resolve could ever enter a man into the spiritual power released only by dependency. Resolve will always dissolve. But by surrender we will never cease to enter.

Why is it this way? It is because God Himself is our salvation (Psalm 38:22). He saved us from a life that doesn't look to Him. Again I say, *"Salvation is the rescue from a life apart from God."* Have we a sensitivity to see that our own life is something so evil, no matter how *"good"* it seems, that we must be saved from it? A life without the Lordship of Christ requires saving! Leonard Ravenhill said, *"The greatest sin in the world… is, 'I can manage my life without God.'"*[23] A life still in our own hands is dead. Paul talked

"If He is to be Lord, He can only ascend to the throne in your life by the bankrupt recognition and surrender of total reliance."

about people being *"dead even while they live"* (1 Timothy 5:6). Jesus told us that only the children enter the Kingdom (Mark 10:14); the poor possess the Kingdom (Matthew 5:3); and the infants have revelation of the Kingdom (Matthew 11:25). Everything in God must hinge upon God. This is why Paul said so boldly, that to lean on any addition to dependency severs you from Christ (Galatians 5:4). There is no other way to have the rule of God truly ruling our lives than for us to declare, *"My soul says, 'You are my Lord.'"* If He is to be Lord, He can only ascend to the throne in your life by the bankrupt recognition and surrender of total reliance. It is unavoidable that utter dependency and absolute surrender are required.

CONCLUSION

Finally, I encourage a meditation upon Luke 21:1-4. This simple, yet moving, short story reveals the severity of poverty like none other. Without poverty there is no totality. Without poverty there is only partiality. The reason that most Christians in the West do not give all that they are over to God is due to the missing element of poverty of soul. The reason why most Christians in the West give partially to God is because they give out of their surplus. *God, return us to the poverty that brings totality and save us from giving to You partially!*

"Anyone who hasn't had an encounter with God, doesn't know God, because God is not a philosophy to be learned but a person to be known....Any revelation from Scripture that doesn't lead us to the person of Jesus Christ only makes us more religious and equips us to argue with those who disagree." ~Bill Johnson

"Oh what enlightenment, what joys, what delight of heart is experienced by that man who has learned to feed on Jesus, and Jesus alone." ~Charles Spurgeon

"Jesus didn't die to make bad men, good men, but to make dead men live." ~Leonard Ravenhill

"Only total surrender brings total communion." ~Benny Hinn

"Rest. The only work you are required to do now is to give your most intense attention to His still, small voice within." ~Madame Guyon

"In vain I sought without, for You who are within." ~St. Augustine

"Violently turn your will over to God." ~François Fénelon

"Remember the one condition; habitual, unceasing dependence upon Him. He must do all." ~Andrew Murray

"Jesus didn't die so He could follow you." ~Francis Chan

CHAPTER 3

BURNING DOVE

*"In the presence of the Lord is fullness of joy
and pleasure forever more."*
~Psalm 16:11

There lies in the midst of Christendom a great danger, a danger that is deeply woven into the fabric of modern American Christianity. It is not as much a danger of doctrinal error as it is an absence of the most vital underlying element of spirituality. The danger is a seed that lacks moisture. Jesus said that the seed would *"wither away"* because of lack of moisture (Luke 8:6). The word *"wither"* is defined as: *"To become dry or shriveled, to cease to flourish, to fall into decay or decline."*[24]

Without the moisture of the Holy Spirit coupled with the seed of the Word, we will empty the realities of the spiritual life of their actuality and cage them behind the bars of theology. The result of which is, a ceasing to flourish, a decaying, and the reduction of a consistent living experience of God, to a dried up black and white doctrinal statement with our name signed at the bottom. Though our words may be correct, without the moisture of His presence, they are empty of that quality of life that comes from above.

Jesus said, *"My words...are Spirit and life"* (John 6:63). This quality of speaking retains within it, for the receiver, the power and incentive to remain clinging to God when everyone else seems to turn away. For the disciples said, *"Where else can we go? You have the words of life"* (John 6:68).

LONGING FOR HIS PRESENCE

"My soul longs for You as a parched land" (Psalm 143:6).

In this particular instance, David does not say, as he did before, *"I thirst for You in a parched land,"* but *"as a parched land."* He likens his very soul to the land that is dry. When a land is parched, it yields no produce, it is dry, and it is dead. David understood that a mind, will, and emotions that are parched, are disconnected from the source of life and consequently fruitfulness.

Every backslider that has ever died in God first died of thirst. Apart from God's presence, there exists no potential for life. Our theological seminaries run the danger of imparting biblical information distanced from a living and vibrant revelation of Jesus Himself. We must look to Him to come and quicken, inspire and breathe, or we will become cerebral retainers instead of spiritual conduits.

There are countless theologians with a vast understanding of the Word of God, yet their souls are severed from the God of the Word. You don't have to be pure to understand what the Bible has recorded, but you must be pure to see God (Matthew 5:8). We must never forget that amazing story of the disciples on the road to Emmaus. I believe that it contains a valuable truth concerning our current subject, it is written, *"...He expounded to them the things concerning Himself in all the Scriptures"* (Luke 24). I used to see that Scripture as a self-evident truth that the Word of God reveals Jesus. Though I do believe that the Scriptures contain the potential to reveal Jesus, I am more inclined to see that particular Scripture in a different light. I feel the Holy Spirit's nudge in my heart, that such an arrangement of words is an indication, not that the Scriptures unlock Jesus, as much as the fact that the presence of Jesus and interaction with Jesus, will unlock the Scriptures. The Lamb is the illumination (Revelation 21:23). HE unlocks the Scriptures to reveal HIMSELF; from glory to glory we see Jesus more and more.

I once had a cat. He knew very well where his food was located, and he could bring himself all the way to the can of "Seafood Delight." He could even touch the can with his paw. I recall him pushing it around the bathroom tile floor. But without me, he could never open it, and in

49

turn could not receive its contents. Without my human superior intelligence and anatomy to aid him, he could only retain the knowledge of where his food was. It is not foolishness to note, that no amount of knowledge concerning the location of food could ever bring any nourishment to his body. We must see the Scriptures in the same light. Without the Holy Spirit, the Bible is unable to give life. As Jesus noted in John 6, *"The Spirit gives life."* Paul had the same understanding, stating, *"...The letter kills, but the Spirit gives life"* (2 Corinthians 3:6).

Though the moral wisdom of the Scriptures is in many ways practical and can be implemented in some fashion, I submit to you, that without the living presence of Jesus to quicken it, it will remain in the brain and never drop into our spirit and allow the person of the Spirit to perform His transforming work. Jesus did not die to make us students, but sons. This is what God is after. He is not into us seeking life by education (John 5:39), nor is it possible to educate ourselves onto the cross. We must become something completely other than what we are. This is the work of the Spirit. This is the reason I believe many believers are stuck in the cycle of ever learning, but never coming to the knowledge of the truth (Titus 3:7). Jesus said, *"I am...the truth..."* (John 14:6). This whole thing is hinged upon knowing God, not knowing about God (John 17:3).

> **"Jesus did not die to make us students, but sons."**

I promise you that nothing is more flammable in hell than a sinful life wrapped up in Bible pages. And to drive the point home even further, without the Holy Spirit, the Bible will never burn.

RECOGNIZING HIS PRESENCE

"Lord, I cry unto Thee, make haste unto me..." (Psalm 141:1). David's cry is for God to come to him. He is not craving the best reader of the law to come fill his ears with truths. He wanted Him who is truth. He is craving, in the midst of his trouble, the nearness of God. He also said, *"The nearness of God is my good"* (Psalm 73:28). David understood the worthless state of man apart from God. Oh, the presence of God in his life was his goodness. Without His presence, there is no goodness, as a *"tree cannot bear forth fruit of itself"* (John 15:4).

The presence of the Lord is the heart of every issue. His presence in our lives is everything (Psalm 62:7). His presence is our distinguishing factor. Israel was just another nation without the presence of God. They would have been destroyed without God's presence fighting for them. In the same way, without His presence we are finished. The Lord Himself is our strength, not our profession in Him. We are not saved by reciting Scriptures, though we do recite Scriptures and will recite the Scriptures; we are saved by Him who is salvation. We are empowered by Him who is strength. Our victory is found standing behind God with His glorious shadow cast over the entire being. We win, when He swings the sword. We are above all things, *"hiders"* (Psalm 31:20).

Moses wouldn't go forward without God's presence. Gideon as one man would deliver the nation because of the presence of the Lord. The prophets stood in and came forth from the presence of the Lord. John's revelation of Jesus was in the presence of the Lord. His presence is literally everything. Without His presence, we are and have nothing. In Revelation, it is only the Lamb who is worthy to open the scroll (Revelation 5:2,4,9,12). He alone unlocks Himself, *"...he that loveth me shall be loved of my Father, and I will love him, and will manifest myself unto him"* (John 14:21).

It is the moisture and the seed together that cause increase and growth. His presence, not theologically or positional, but the actual undeniable experienced presence of God, is the rain upon the dead, barren, and dry land of our souls. His living and abiding presence is our good. He, Himself, is our hiding place (Psalm 119:114). He, Himself, is our refuge (Psalm 142:5). It is the shelter from the beating sun of life. A man would be a fool to think that by reminding himself of the location of a physical shelter that he is actually under it. His presence is a living reality. It is a blissful ecstasy. It is a wonderful experiential actuality that is full of joy. It is full of pleasure, always. He actually is a *"river of delights"* (Psalm 36:8). A.W. Tozer said, *"God is a shoreless sea of pleasure."*[25] There is a literal continual experience that moved David to pen, *"Better is one day in Your house than thousands elsewhere..."* (Psalm 84:10).

"I love the habitation of Your house – the place where Your glory dwells" (Psalm 26:8). *"One thing I have asked from the LORD, that I shall seek: That I may dwell in the house of the LORD all the days of my life, to behold the beauty of the LORD, and to meditate in His temple"* (Psalm 27:4). It was Robert Murray McCheyne who said, *"A calm hour with God is worth a lifetime with any man."*[26]

His presence was the secret to the endurance of the martyrs. As Thomas A. Kempis wrote, *"When Jesus is with us, NOTHING seems difficult,"* for it was through the empowering presence of the Spirit that Jesus gave Himself up (Hebrews 9:14). The presence of the Spirit is the detachment from the physical reign. He is grace, and grace is our new reigning master (Hebrews 10:29; Romans 5:21; Philippians 2:13). Though we still feel the pull of the natural desires, we see them from an eagle's eye view and any of their activity is only through a consciously permitted rebellious chosen subjectivity; because all grace for Godliness is available all the time for everything (1 Corinthians 9:8).

I submit to you that the chief danger in Christianity is to be without this daily living experience of our God through fellowship with His Spirit (2 Corinthians 13:14; Philippians 2:1). Without this daily living experience of God, we reduce

"I submit to you that the chief danger in Christianity is to be without this daily living experience of our God."

this New Life from knowing God by divine interaction with Him, to church membership, Scripture knowledge, and "prayer time," and we believe that this is "knowing God." We begin to emphasize a change we want to see on the outside, instead of receiving Him continually on the inside. We can easily slip into an emphasis on social justice in the stead of our Saving Jesus.

When the ark of the presence was at the home of Obed-Edom, literally, everything flourished in his life (2 Samuel 6). So it is with knowing God; the flourishing of your spiritual life will be in exact proportion to the attention you give to His presence in your life. Only when His presence is the centerpiece of our lives, can He make our lives His masterpiece. *"Never let anything get bigger in your consciousness than the awareness of His presence..."* (Bill Johnson).[27] It was William C. Burns who wrote, *"Many who do come into the secret place... enter it and leave it just as they entered, without ever so much as realizing the presence of God. And there are some believers who, even when they do obtain...quickening of soul, leave the secret place without seeking more."*

I woke up one morning and went into my prayer closet. In the midst of stillness, the Lord spoke to my heart concerning this great desire He has for His people to be His habitation and for them to make Him their habitation. Jesus said, *"Abide in Me and I in you...."* A power outlet and plug are two pieces that must come into one another for the flow of electricity. He covers us and we go into Him. How He longs for us to savor, respect, protect, cherish, and honor His presence.

There are four short keys that I believe will aid us in abiding in His presence, the first of which is LIVING FOR HIS PRESENCE. We must wake up every day and remember that this day has been given to us, above all things, to enjoy our God. No matter what task is standing before us, we must adjust our soul's disposition to see that our first priority is to live for His presence.

The second key is to LIVE IN HIS PRESENCE. We must consciously abide in that inner place where the Spirit's presence is known and experienced. In order to do this, we must live a collected life. The major attack upon the abiding place is scatteredness. The devil knows that if he can scatter your soul it will not be still enough to plug into the socket of life. Our job is to simply plug into the wall. God's job is the infusion of power. Infusion is when the properties of one become useful in another. It is when two different things become one. To live in His presence, we must remain settled in Him by worship and surrender. If at all we feel the scattering of the soul, we must turn within by worship and surrender till the soul is stilled and plugged into the infusion of His Spirit in our spirit—the residence of divine glory. Benny Hinn said, *"Every time you worship, you inhale heaven."*[28] This is what He is after in the reconciliation, us in Him and Him in us. ONENESS. *"What our Lord did was done with this intent, and this alone, that He might be with us and we with Him."*[29]

"The disciple must retract his soul into the place of surrender before he can be led. "

The third key is to LIVE AROUND HIS PRESENCE. I suggest this to mean that we make every decision of our lives, moments, and days around the fact that we are living for, and in, His presence. How many things that are eating our lives away on a daily basis would be set to the side if we looked at every decision in life from the desire to maximize our reception of God?

The fourth is to LIVE FROM HIS PRESENCE. Our counsel, words, preaching, life, and presence will carry life if they are issued from a life that is living in the presence of God. Bill Johnson said, *"We will always release that which we are aware of."* We must remain in His presence, consciously and experientially, and allow everything that we are to flow from that river within. The most honest man will confess that there is no other way to live quickened by divine life but to rejoice always, pray without ceasing, be thankful in everything, love one another, live in peace, be patient, genuinely kind, always self-controlled, let your gentleness be known to all, and be faithful without such a continual flow of His presence in our lives.

REST

Jesus said, *"Come to Me...I will give you rest"* (Matthew 11:28). Isaiah 63:14 shows us that after the beasts are brought down, the Holy Spirit gave them *"rest"* in the wilderness from which *"He lead them."* The leading of the Holy Spirit is in the place of rest. No rest, no leading. No leading, no following. No following, no life. He is *"the way, the truth, and the life"* (John 14:6). He leads us in the way, which makes us know the truth, and fills and animates us with the life. Jesus said, *"If you continue in My Word, then you are truly My disciples."* The disciple must retract his soul into the place of surrender before he can be led. As Madame Guyon wrote in her amazing book, *A Short and Easy Method of Prayer*, *"...it is a sweet sinking into deity."* The Scripture states, *"...put on Christ* (Romans 13:11). The word used for *"put"* is actually better translated *"sink into."* It is surrender. It is yielding. It is not an effort to act but a ceasing to act, that He may act.

This rest is a place of transcendence above efforts and striving. Rest is the ceasing of our Adamic[30] outflow and the quickening that comes from a genuine inflow of God. It is the ceasing of striving, which infuses us with revelation. *"**Be still** and **know** that I am God"* (Psalm 46:10). It is the ceasing of our Adamic outflow that enables His divine inflow. Jesus said, *"...but the Father who dwells in Me, does His works"* (John 14:10). This is rest. Man, ceasing from his own initiative and resting in the empowerment of the Holy Spirit within him; yielding to His direction and consequently finding the animation of divine life. This is the end of man's own efforts and the beginning of authentic divine enablement. This is sonship.

SONSHIP

Jesus said, *"I do nothing on my own initiative"* (John 8:28). This is the perfect description of a life of rest, waiting and being led by the quickening life of God. I have seen that the words "rest" and "waiting" are synonymous in the spiritual life. Waiting is not an inactive life, but the activation of divine life. It is the quickening with heavenly power through the rejection of our earthly initiative.

Robert Gladstone described this uncreated life as, *"the divine quality of existence."*[31] This new covenant of grace is so much higher than the old covenant of law. We are so far beyond rules and laws. Grace places us in a higher system of existence. We are not born into a new way of trying to obey the law, but a genuinely spiritual life.

"Waiting is not an inactive life, but the activation of divine life." If a man came to an angel and tried to bribe him with money, the angel might look at him and say, *"What am I going to do with that? I am from a completely other system of existence. Your money means nothing to me."* In the same way, we have entered a higher system of existence, so as to render the seductions of this worthless and therefore powerless. We don't live for our own independent lives, but by and through divine life. In fact, the two can never join together. If a man lives for his own life, he cannot partake of divine life. When a man receives divine life, he has renounced his own life.

"Man's actions should not be governed by a sense of right or wrong, but by obedience."[32] What kind of obedience? It is obedience to the leading of the Spirit of God. *"Those that are led by the Spirit are the sons of God* (Romans 8). Jesus

is the *"firstborn among many brethren."* God's desire is to *"bring many sons to glory."* Charles Finney said, *"Cherish the slightest impressions from the Holy Ghost."* Sonship is the call; *"God has sown the cross into the earth to reap sons."*[33] From the beginning, God's heart for humanity has been the same: to share with them the union that He shares with His Son. But He will form these sons by offering to them this life and giving them the opportunity to reject it. He sets before us life and death and desires for us to choose life (Joshua 24).

There are always two trees in the Garden: the tree of the knowledge of good and evil, and the tree of life. There must be two trees for the formation of character. Life is not inevitable. Oswald Chambers said, *"I cannot live holy. But I can decide to let Jesus make me holy."*[34] The choice in the Christian life is to choose between being satisfied with knowing what is right and wrong and live accordingly or be quickened by a higher life and ruled by the power of the Spirit (Romans 8). Our law is the *"Law of the Spirit"* (Romans 8:2). This is so foreign to most believers today that it sounds like a fairy tale to tell someone that God *"...will give you a new heart and a new Spirit and cause you to walk in My (His) ways"* (Ezekiel 36:26).

"Jesus was completely led because He was completely given to the Spirit's leading."

The presence of the Spirit is a holy life. The Greek word that Jesus used to describe the Holy Spirit has many meanings. Jesus said, *"The Comforter will come"* (John 14). This word means: partner, teacher, leader, guide, advocate, strengthener, standby, helper, intercessor, comforter, and counselor. He performs it. Jesus, one with the Spirit and emptied of Himself, was totally sensitive to the slightest impressions from the Holy Spirit. Jesus was completely led because He was completely given to the Spirit's leading. A partial offering will never bring a complete fire. Herein lies the reason most American Christians are cold and not consumed with God — the reason why young people prefer video games to prayer and movies to the Word of God. A partial offering is never consumed. *"Our God is a consuming fire"* (Hebrews 12). Meaning, He only descends upon something He can totally destroy. Partiality lacks vitality. He has not ceased to be an All-Consuming Fire. He is simply *"looking at barren altars with nothing to set on fire."*[35] Sonship is a human soul wholly taken up into God.

"No matter what has been presented to us in all of its grandeur and intellectual brilliance, if it is not soaked in God Himself, it is just as empty as any other religion."

The totality of a life laid down is the ignition of this divine rest, the essence of waiting, the heart of Spirit-leading, divine life, and a consumed life of fire. We are under the influence of the Spirit to the degree that He fills us. He fills us to the degree we are empty of ourselves. Jesus said, *"If any man would come after Me, let him deny himself"* (Matthew 16:24), because He knew it was the only way to be completely under the influence of the Spirit and dominated by God. *"The only right a Christian has is the right to give up his rights."*[36] It is in that renunciation that we find resurrection.

SPIRIT LIFE

We don't stop going after God to find rest; we press into Him who is rest to enter rest. Rest is spelled, J-E-S-U-S. The tree doesn't focus on bearing fruit, but on receiving the sap. We cannot pin fruit on the tree. It will just fall off. Not only that, it is a farce. Hypocrisy is empty, plastic fruit pinned on the tree by the efforts of man's hands in the stead of genuine organic outflow of a lively reception of the proper nutrients. Real fruit, in the life of a believer, only issues out of an inward connection with the life of God. This inward connection is cultivated and received in no other place than spending time with and abiding in God; waiting in His presence for His voice to enter and quicken us with a revelation of Himself, and from this place, walking behind, Him constantly aware of His presence and leading. Psalm 28:1 shows us that without His voice coming in to us our lives will digress to looking like the wicked. Robert Gladstone used to tell us in Bible school, *"If we don't live by revelation, we don't live."* It is written that, *"Man shall not live by bread alone, but by every word that proceeds out of the mouth of God"* (Deuteronomy 8:3).

This is the higher life. *"The mind set on the Spirit is life and peace"* (Romans 6:4; Isaiah 26:3). This is Christianity. No matter what has been presented to us in all of its grandeur and intellectual brilliance, if it is not soaked in the living reality of God Himself, it is just as empty as any other religion; an adherence to principles and efforts for outward modification without an inward transformation. Bill Johnson said, *"To desire principles over presence, is to desire a kingdom without the King."*[37] In no other religion does one's God enter into the man who receives Him and then after entering him, He performs His works through that man who yields to Him and then rewards that man for the works that he did. There is nothing like God. How wonderful He is! Our character in God is measured by our ability to surrender to Him. One man said it like this, *"The greatness of a man's power is measured by his surrender."*[38] Our ceasing to be is our greatness, for it makes us a channel of God's life. This truth is to permeate every area of life. In the secret place of fellowship with the Holy Spirit, we should not come with a list to pray through. We are waiters on His life. We are after His heart. We want His quickening. I am not interested in trying to do what I think is best. I want His divine orchestration. I want to move in concert with the Holy Spirit, who is a person. Do you?

INTIMACY

There is intimacy with God: *"Know that He has set apart him that is godly for Himself"* (Psalm 4). *"The intimacy of the Lord is for those who fear Him"* (Psalm 25:14). Can our finite minds grasp such a glorious separation? Can we fathom such an attachment to God? God has chosen to set aside a man apart from the others, *"For*

Himself"? Proverbs 8 tells us that, *"I love those who love Me."* Though God loves the world (John 3:16), never doubt that there is a special place in His heart and a wonderful, intimate union for those who give themselves wholly to Him. Do

> *"Above all, we must be a people completely distanced from everything in this world by reason of absolute satisfaction with our God."*

you recall the specific note penned out by the writer of Hebrews, quoting the Old Testament psalm, *"He has loved righteousness and hated wickedness, and therefore I have anointed Him above His fellows"*? Your heart towards God can set you apart from others. In the book of Samuel, God says that He found someone *"better"* than Saul (1 Samuel 15:28). There is a *"better,"* and it is connected with an obedience that is *"better"* than sacrifice. Hearing God and obeying Him is more valuable to God than all the religious acts that can be done for Him combined. Abraham was called God's friend (James 2:23). Daniel was a man greatly loved. Moses was the most humble man on the earth and spoke with God as a man speaks to his friend. One of the greatest statements ever recorded in the Scriptures out of the mouth of God concerning a man is about Job, *"There is none like him in all the earth"* (Job 1). Read that last statement again. God said that about a human. David alone was called, *"A man after God's own heart"* (Acts 13:22). John the Apostle was called the one *"whom Jesus loved."* These things are not written so that we would know they existed, but that we might aspire to be that man also.[39] Leonard Ravenhill said, *"No one can change God's opinion of you but you."* No one can love God for you. No one can seek God for you; just as no one sets my alarm for me to wake up before the sun to stare into the face of the Son. Intimacy is choosing to refuse to look into the face of life without first having looked into the face of God: *"Seek my face. Your face Lord, will I seek"* (Psalm 27:8).

WAITING

I believe one of the surest signs of intimacy with God is waiting on God in His presence. Waiting on God is the secret to spiritual strength. Why? Because waiting on God is the route of death to our initiative and the quickening of the initiative of God. Our lives should be marked as waiting lives (Psalm 25:5). Though Jesus did nothing on His own initiative (John 8:28), He simply laid it down (John 10:18). The one thing our initiative is good for is to be laid on the altar of sacrifice. Waiting on God is the refusal of our Adamic initiative and the trust in His divine wind to sweep in and carry us into the heights of spiritual activity.

How do we activate the divine strength of God? Waiting.
"Wait on the Lord...He shall strengthen thine heart" (Psalm 27:14).
"Because of His strength will I wait..." (Psalm 59:9).
"They that wait upon the Lord shall renew their strength..." (Isaiah 40:31).

How do we short-circuit the strength of God? Don't wait.

"He who hurries his footsteps errs..." (Proverbs 19:2).

"Everyone who is hasty comes surely to poverty" (Proverbs 21:5).

Spending time waiting upon God in His presence is the training ground for the spiritual life.

- You learn to hear His voice.
- You learn to feel His impressions.
- You begin to experience His heart.
- You sharpen your vision.
- You get aligned with His thoughts and heart.
- Above all, you are fulfilled and satisfied with Him.

Spending time with God is the absolute core of life in God. Without this time of diligently entering His rest we will die! Unless we wait upon the Lord, **"No one can love God for you. No one can seek God for you."** we will remain drawing from our own reservoir, which is dead empty. We will wither away. The Gospel taps us into rest, but we have to be diligent to abide therein. The ground for an abiding life is the secret life. We should never eclipse the secret place with the abiding place, and never eclipse the abiding place with the secret place. They work together and constitute an unbroken communion with God's Spirit.

Hebrews 4 shows us the divine paradox of diligently entering His rest. The rest is then laid out as trust (absolute surrender to Jesus) and obedience (the only outflow of such a disposition). It is as simple as salvation. Colossians tells us, "...*as you received Him, so walk in Him*" (Colossians 2:6).

Leonard Ravenhill said it like this, "*A man first collapses in the prayer closet.*"[40] Meaning, if a man has fallen in his life, he first failed to fall on his knees for strength. E.M. Bounds said, "*The devil trembles when he sees the weakest saint upon his knees.*"[41] Why? Because he knows that he has gone to "*fetch strength against him.*" I tell you that, "*A man who is intimate with God will never be intimidated by man*" (Ravenhill).[42] A man whose face is set on God's face will never shrink from the face of a devil.

This subject is vitally important. Those who chose to diligently come to Jesus and wait on Him access the rest of God. Those who give Him their initiative apprehend the power of God. God gives His initiative to those who give Him their initiative. The divine wind of God only lifts up the wings of the one who waits for His gust. The rest is the Spirit. The Spirit is our rest. The Spirit of God leads and guides, strengthens and enables. Paul said in Galatians chapter 5, "*If you walk in the Spirit, you will not gratify the desires of sinful nature.*" What he is saying is, "*If you wait for the enablement of the Spirit, you will never fail.*"

What confidence! He knew the rest. He knew the dominance of the Spirit. He knew that it was above efforts and striving. He knew that in the rest, there is only victory. It is the place of hiding *"under the shadow of the Almighty"* (Psalm 91). It is the place of which David said, *"O God, my strength"* (Psalm 18:1); *"You are my hiding place"* (Psalm 32:7). Waiting prayer, which is submitting to the leading of the Spirit, is the air of the Christian life. *"When we cease to pray, we quench the Spirit. When we quench the Spirit, we cease to pray"* (Benny Hinn).[43] I would add, if we don't wait on His lead, we quench the Spirit. It was Heidi Baker who said, *"Prayer is air."*[44]

The revolution of prayer in the Christian life is a major evidence of the infilling of the Spirit. *"Spending time with Jesus is number one. Don't ever forget that"* (David Hogan);[45] *"To be much for God, we must be much alone with God"* (Leonard Ravenhill).

Spending time with God is our sap for fruit and our air for breathing. It is the heart of victory. It is our power for living. Without it, we will die just as sure as a fish out of water. We will become increasingly more worldlier. We will lose our sense of conviction. We will lose sight of our spiritual purpose. We will begin to ooze the poison of the first Adam, instead of the life of the last (1 Corinthians 15:45). We will cease to find all our satisfaction in God and by default seek satisfaction elsewhere.

Above all, we must be a people completely distanced from everything in this world by reason of absolute satisfaction with our God. When we look to other things to satisfy us, we testify to the world that God is not enough.

The greatest witness is the man who is most satisfied with His God. God fulfills all the longings of the soul. That is His satisfaction. Jesus came to the woman at the well looking for something from her. When she questioned Him about it, Jesus revealed to her that the real thirst of His heart was to quench her thirst by giving her living water that will forever satisfy her soul. I submit to you that God's thirst is to be the one to quench our thirst. We quench God's thirst and meet His desires when we allow God to be the complete satisfaction of our thirst and desire. Only a waiting life knows such things, because he experiences them, while the school masters scratch their heads and wonder what such an internal phenomenon is all about.

STILLNESS

The inward surrender of a fixed and sustained, full attention upon God, waiting in worship, is the only way into the presence of God. David said, *"To You I lift up my soul"* (Psalm 143:8). His mind, will, and emotions were laid upon the altar unto God. As a cup could never be filled as it spins on the table, so our spinning souls must get still before God for Him to flow into us. Madame Guyon said, *"God dwells in absolute stillness."*[46] There is no other place in which to meet Him.

We must remember that just because we are quiet, doesn't mean we are still. Stillness is the soul laid upon the altar of God in worshipful, wholehearted fixation upon God Himself, anticipating the impartation of His life-giving words into your spirit (Psalm 4:4). This is the disposition of waiting to be exercised in prayer and lived in, in the world. We can live still. As the external man moves, the internal man has stilled himself into the highest quality of actions by Spirit-quickened life. Jesus lived this way.

We know very little about what is going on while we are on the earth; it is imperative that the Holy Spirit, in prayer, leads us. He knows what is going on. Listen to Him. You will not hear Him in any other place than worship, waiting, and wholehearted attention. *"Retire frequently with Him into the inner chamber of the heart, where the gentle voice of the Spirit is only heard if all is still"* (Andrew Murray, *Abide In Christ*).

Some use music, a certain prayer or phrase, or some kind of aid to focus completely upon God. But I believe the greatest aid to stillness is silence in solitude. Once you are fixed upon God, you must be sure to sustain your full attention upon Him in wor-

> *"Stillness is the soul laid upon the altar of God in worshipful, wholehearted fixation upon God Himself."*

ship, not necessarily with words, but definitely with a wholehearted surrender of love toward Him. This will cause you to become aware of His nearness that is always with you (Hebrews 13:8). This is the base for all of what God wants to accomplish in your time with Him. Here is the dispensing of the most vital nutrients for spiritual life. His inflow of peace beyond all understanding and complete fulfillment in the most vulnerable parts of man is the overwhelming satisfaction that transcends anything else that exists. This is where the Scriptures will come alive. Remember in Luke 24, it was only in His presence that the Word of God revealed Jesus, *"He expounded to them...."* The presence of God is the key to the Scriptures because they are locked until He opens them.

From this base of an inward setting of yourself upon Him, prayer becomes a powerfully rich experience, both of your heart's releasing to God and His guiding you by His Spirit in seeing the desires of His heart. Prayer will come alive. And there is simply nothing like it. Nothing touches its caliber of fulfillment and life. You can really tell when a man has touched God in prayer. He becomes addicted to the experience of interacting with God in prayer and he is latched on to his God throughout the day. Even if you don't naturally understand what is happening to you in this stillness, be assured you are becoming like Him.

It is here that He gets you to drink from the river of His delights (Psalm 36:8). Just as a man cannot drink from the river while he is moving, so the soul must stop its activities for him to drink from this wonderful, fulfilling river of God that He has granted unlimited access to. But, stopping is only the beginning, because worship must transcend expression and become reception or it is of little value. No amount of external contact with the river can quench the inward thirst of the soul. We must drink.

Waiting in His presence is renewing and faith building as you cease your outflow and subject yourself to His inflow and leading. It is this submission that releases you from the bondage of your own thinking. It makes you a subject and not the leader, respecting the Holy Spirit as the leader. We must be *"led by the Spirit."*

"Without His presence I don't stand a chance." I know this one thing. Without His presence I don't stand a chance. Neither do you. It is not God's plan. He wants everything to hinge upon Him. The oneness of God and man, what reconciliation! This is God's desire. Worship; *the inward fixation of the soul sustained upon God, suspended in worship and total surrender, waiting upon Him and His voice.* This is the divine melting of the soul of man into the Spirit of God where the burning dove is free to be Himself and men start to look like Jesus. *"...above all else, let us be much alone with Jesus"* (Charles Spurgeon).[47]

" If you long for God, you will hate the things of this world; if you love the things of this world, you will not long for God." ~Benny Hinn

"I was dying of thirst. When my spiritual eyes were open I saw the rivers of living water flowing from His pierced side. I drank of it and was satisfied. I have always drunk of that water of life and never thirst in the sandy desert of this world." ~Sadhu Sundar Singh

"God longs to be longed for and seeks to be sought." ~A.W. Tozer

"My soul followeth hard after you." ~David

"My soul clings to you." ~David

"…Oh this pleasing pain. It makes my soul press after God." ~David Brainerd

"There's more, friends. But we just want to skip a day of food and maybe turn off the TV once or twice a week to meet with God more and we think the glory is going to come down. Can you really say, 'God, I am desperate'? We are not talking about saving room for dessert, but holy starvation." ~Dr. Michael L. Brown

CHAPTER 4

BURNING THIRST

"I shall seek You earnestly; My soul thirsts for You, my flesh yearns for You, In a dry and weary land where there is no water." ~Psalm 63:1

Brothers and sisters, is your soul thirsty for God? Is there an inward burning in the pit of your stomach that thrusts your soul into a groaning prayer to be totally dominated by God? Are you arrested at times throughout the day with a tearful yearning for more of God? Is the perfect satisfaction of His presence in your life urging you with the reality that there is so much more of Him to possess? Is He daily drawing your heart to know Him more? This is what David is oozing out of his heart when he writes, *"My soul thirsts for You."*

DESPERATE CRIES

One ordinary night in the men's dormitory at the Brownsville Revival School of Ministry in 1999, I went into the bathroom to brush my teeth before the lights were to be turned out. I saw three of my friends in the bathroom talking about Jesus. I joined the conversation and we began to talk about a strange burning, yearning for more of God. Recalling some of the giants of the faith that had entered Him so deeply, we felt moved to pray. As we prayed, there was a touch of the Holy Spirit tangible to us. When we finished praying we sensed Him so strongly that no one wanted to move, so we decided to pray again. In the blink of an eye something happened. We were overwhelmed with desperation for a greater oneness with the Holy Spirit. It was so intense upon our hearts that one of the men thrust himself to the floor, releasing from his guts what sounded like bellowing hell cries. I remember looking at him thinking, *"Something supernatural has gripped him."*

"We should live longing for God." At that moment I was hit with a sensation inside likened unto being punched in the stomach "by the air" and I fell to my knees, gripped with uncontainable, bursting love for Jesus and desire to love Him more. My heart felt like liquid love mixed with an overwhelming sense that I barely knew Him. The reality of what is available of Him to me had ignited a groaning deep in my innermost parts. I couldn't do anything but cry and let out what seemed like a curdling, straining of every muscle of my body, scream that could only be held for about eight seconds. I held it out as long as I could and then lay in this glorious presence until I had enough strength to do it again. It seemed to be the only thing that could satisfy this deep, desperate God craving that was gripping my soul.

I remember, as I was on the ground, feeling my own saliva dripping down onto my hands, as I cared nothing for what I looked like. I must have looked like an animal with rabies that was just run over by a jeep. I blacked out at one point. I don't know how long I was out, but I opened my eyes only to see the whole bathroom full of about thirty guys with the same thing happening to them. The screams in that bathroom sounded like a "weeping and gnashing" hell. I am sorry to use such terms in connection with such holy things, but it seems to be the only way to properly create a picture for you to see in your inner eye what I saw that night. Men were pounding their fists onto the tile floor and hammering the wood bench with their arms, like wild chimpanzees locked in a room that was on fire. Some were so worn out from crying and screaming that they just lay there in the ecstasy of His loving presence.

Even writing this now, my eyes flood with tears. It was a glorious moment in time, where God's dying love for man was placed in our souls for Him and we couldn't hold it. It turned us into what looked like wild beasts and blacked-out college students drunk with the wine from heaven. I would have thought the whole thing demonic had I not felt the glorious presence of a living God who penetrates our hearts with His love.

I remember that the leadership asked us to move from the bathroom to the music room. I was so drunk and weak and delirious, but I can still see the weeping faces of the two men carrying me to, what turned into, an all-night glorious desperation surge for God in the music room.

"...when God the Holy Spirit comes close, all vacuums of the soul cease up." Though I know that such an experience is rare, there should be a longing that is constantly arising from our hearts for God alone. We love to try to get God to look at things, but God is longing for the one who will simply look at Him. We have so many side issues today that it seems so foreign to just want God. Every morning when I rise for early-morning prayer, I have special things that I say to Him, one of which is this, *"I am not here to get You to do anything. I am not here to ask You for anything. I am not here because I need to be. I am not here because I have to be. I am here just because I want You; Your presence and Your voice. I am only here to experience Your presence and hear Your voice. From there the rest will come."*

THE LONGING LIFE

We should live longing for God. He longs for us and as we surrender to Him, His longing for us will take us into longing for Him. I see danger signs when I go weeks without being arrested by an inward desire for Him that moves my soul to tears. When I see such a danger sign, I respond by repentance and fasting, locking myself away with Him until that fountain of a broken, sensitive heart is flowing

"The sad fact is that so many Christians live their lives not satisfied with God."

again. It shouldn't be uncommon that our love for Jesus erupts in our hearts and bursts out of our eyes in tears. This is hunger for God. I have seen that shutting myself away with Him daily and for extended periods, frequently coupled with fasting, really helps me maintain such distance from myself, and burning love for Him, just as all relationships are fueled by communication time alone with each other. I also noticed that worldly tolerations cool down my love for Jesus. It was John Wesley who said, *"Anything that cools my love for God is the world."*[48]

Maybe you feel bad reading this because you have never experienced such things. Well, I tell you that they are glorious and irreplaceable and that they are for you. They are God's desire for you. He wants you, above all things, to want Him. Call on His name today in a solitary place and say, *"God, I want to want You! Make me hungry for You! I want to hunger only for Your presence."*

I remember Benny Hinn saying, *"If you have ten minutes to pray, take nine to worship."*[49] It was A.W. Tozer who said, *"Worship is the inward gaze of the soul upon God."*[50] I start out every day of my life with the Holy Spirit alone; the first hour or two is just stillness of worship, giving Him all my affection and attention, waiting, while simply gazing upon Him. Another statement I say to Him every morning and multiple times throughout the day is this, *"I give You all my attention and I worship You. I am not here to pray for people or to ask You for anything. I just want You. Take me up into Yourself. I give You everything."*

Man is an endless succession of cravings. He wants things, fulfillments, gratifications, and social stimulations as well as visual stimulations. He is continually reaching out like a many-hosed vacuum. But when God the Holy Spirit comes close, all vacuums of the soul cease up. God is the ultimate fulfillment.

The sad fact is that so many Christians live their lives not satisfied with God. He is our refuge. Our refuge is a person, finding shelter in interaction with God. We need to ask ourselves, have I given something else first place in my heart? The only transaction with God is your life for His.

Ask yourself, *"Do I run to Him?"* If not, *"What do I run to?"*

Ask yourself, *"Do I want Him?"* If not, *"What do I want?"*

Ask yourself, *"Do I live in interaction with Him as the shelter from myself and the collapsing world?"* If not, *"What do I live for?"*

Ask yourself if you have used other things that were more familiar or seemed to be more delightful to your soul as a refuge and satisfaction. Though I understand we are living in this world and have many things that must be done, we must hear His heart asking for all of us. We must see that we are wanted before we can want Him. His poured-out blood and broken body are never-ending evidence that He wants you and me.

Brother, if you would rather watch a movie than rest in His presence, something is wrong. You can repair it today! If you would rather get together with friends and hear their voices than get with God and hear His

"His poured-out blood and broken body are never-ending evidence that He wants you and me."

voice, something is wrong. You can change this today! Anything that is a cloud in the way of your all-out pursuit of God is an obstacle between His love entering your heart. All that He is after in your life are those things that come between you and Him.

DISCIPLINED DILIGENCE

You can make a decision with David, *"Earnestly I will seek You."* The phrase *"I will"* shows me that he *"willed"* to do this. He made up his mind: *"I will seek You."* As a choice of his will, he sought the Lord. He also describes how his determination will manifest itself, using the word, *"Earnestly...."* The translation of this word into English from Hebrew has two meanings. One – *"Earnestly,"* which implies diligence.

Two – *"Early,"* which implies first place or even discipline. His seeking after the Lord in passionate cries is *diligent, disciplined,* and *first priority,* all of which are the natural outcome of a burning heart for God, the way to a burning heart for God, and the sustaining of a burning heart for God. Remember that it is not in our hands to do anything but to make the decision to seek Him. He will empower us. He is the leader and the strength of our life. We look to Him and He does the rest. Our only job is to run to Him. David is saying, *"You, Yourself, are the place that I run for shelter and life. Not things about You, around You, but You, Yourself"* (Presence and Person).

"He wants you to be wholly satisfied in Him. " God asks us to seek His face (Psalm 27:8) and we can make a decision to do so (Psalm 27:8). David also stated, *"I have fixed my heart"* (Psalm 57:7). The most powerful and most victorious resolve we have is when we lay our swords down and let God swing His sword. How do we do this? We look at Him with all our attention in worship. When you are in doubt, turn your eyes on Him. When you are in temptation, turn your eyes to Him. When you have spare time, turn your eyes to Him. We should live, *"looking unto Jesus"* (Romans 12:1). It may be difficult at first to practice such a way of unself-conscious living, but it will soon produce a thirst in the soul, which is satisfied and maintained by the reception of the light of God. *"They looked to the Lord and are radiant"*

(Psalm 34). What reflection of the glory beams from the face that is staring into the light of His face!

"My soul thirsts for You, my body longs for You...." The directing of his will, passionately toward the Lord, resulting in a priority and diligent and disciplined seeking of God, was rooted in none other than an *inward thirst for God.*

ONLY JESUS

Today is a great day to ask yourself, *"Am I really hungry for Jesus and only Jesus?"* One of the main issues in modern Christianity is that though we "love Jesus," we don't love only Jesus. A.W. Tozer, in *The Pursuit of God,* said that the issue in many lives is the "AND." It is the additions to God in the Christian life that snuff Him out. We live our lives and God is allowed in as a part, instead of the source of our life. David Ravenhill said, *"Nothing is more likely to lead to error or heresy than to focus on part rather than the whole."* I would add that nothing is more likely to lead us away from Jesus than to offer part rather than the whole.

Is Christ our life? Even in the midst of work and family, does our heart ache for Jesus? Does the All-Consuming Fire consume us? He wants to be our thirst quencher! If we would only lead people to God as the source of satisfaction, they would be led directly into life. First Peter 3:18 says, *"...the just for the unjust that He might bring us to God."* For He alone can satisfy the longing of the soul (Psalm 107:9).

He seeks to truly be our supreme desire! Above all else, He wants to be all-in-all to us. Do we know what we are apart from the power of God's presence in our lives? Are we burning with thirst?

Once we experience God, other fulfillments are a joke, laughable and even ridiculous next to the power of His presence that is available to us at any time. David described his thirst as a physical craving. He craved God so much that his actual body felt his longing for God.

Oh, if I could tattoo this on your soul—this is what He wants from us above everything—He wants you to be wholly satisfied with Him. He wants to be the total object of your love. *"I am married unto you"* (Jeremiah 3:14). He has given you His affections and commitment. *"...the love of a husband is but a faint picture of the flame which burns in the heart of Jesus. Passing all human union is the mystical cleaving to the Church, for which Christ left His Father, and became one flesh with her."*[51]

With all the tenderness I have, I tell you, anyone who spends more time in front of a TV than before the Lord knows nothing of the thirst to which David is referring. Anyone who wastes his time on meaningless, selfish living, knows nothing of what is pouring out of David's heart. Today, you can turn around. As you read this chapter, you can turn your heart away from vain things of time and look to Him alone.

We can tell everyone how much we *"love His presence and His voice"* and they may believe us, but the truth is this…most of us only love His presence when we stumble upon Him, not enough to go after Him or sincerely, relentlessly abide in Him who burns away all other things that are not Himself. Most of us say that He is life to us, but only come away from everything to sit with Him periodically. If you continually come to Him and experience the fulfillment of God, this life and all it offers will continually dissolve into nothingness. He alone is fulfillment. His purpose alone is purpose. The book of Acts tells us that David *"fulfilled the purpose of God in his generation."* It was His longing for God alone that carried Him into such an attainment. We will fulfill our purpose to the degree we long for Him. If we do not long for Him we will short-circuit the divine system for our lives.

> *"If we do not long for Him we will short-circuit the divine system for our lives."*

NOTHING ELSE CAN SATISFY

David said that his thirst for God was, *"…in a dry and weary land where there is no water."* David's imagery here is perfect! In the last chapter we looked at David as a dry land. In this particular instance, the land that he is describing himself in is *"dry"* and *"weary."* It has no water. It doesn't have the necessities to sustain life. Therefore what is found in this land is worthless, vain, and empty. As Psalm 4:2 says, *"How long will you love what is worthless?"*

The *"dry and weary land"* of this world is death and leads to death. Nothing in this world can satisfy David's thirst but God. He cannot draw from the things of this world and meet his burning thirst, simply because, this world, things, and people cannot produce God. He understood this spiritual wisdom; God alone fulfills. Fulfillment alone is God. God alone is life.

Dear reader, thirst for Him alone! Recognize that this world has nothing for you. Really! Not just because it is what we are supposed to say, but because your soul testifies to such satisfaction in Him that produces thirst for Him. Money, friends, fame, religion, Christianity, materials, pastimes, sports, entertainment, and all the things of this world *are a dry and weary land where there is no water.* Come to Him for Him alone. He will meet you here. God will fulfill your life.

If you have been giving yourself to things that are not Him, simply turn to Him now. In failure, do not turn away from Him. If you have been playing a religious game of devotion, unsatisfied because you are far from His nearness, turn to Him today and experience Him. If you have things that you would rather do than sit with Him, turn to Him today, noticing that this is a sickness in your soul that only His voice can heal. *"When a man is sick, the first thing that goes is his hunger. Lack of spiritual hunger is a sign of spiritual sickness."*[52]

If your Christianity is doing your best to follow a book, pray prayers, and worship on a Sunday morning, and you are not walking above sin and in a continual revelation of His beauty through the fellowship of His Spirit, I submit to you that you have yet to enter the doorway to life.

Dear reader, let your life go and surrender to God, fully. He should be our highest life. We will experience Him to the degree we give ourselves to Him. Not because He is holding back, but because nothing else will empty our soul in order for our soul to be filled with Him. Shakespeare, speaking of love, wrote, *"How weary, stale, flat, and unprofitable seem to me, all the things of this world."* Love blinds to the lesser lovers.

Charles Finney said, *"...we should represent religion as it really is — as living above the world, as consisting in a heavenly mind, as that which gives an enjoyment so spiritual and heavenly as to render the low pursuits and joys of worldly men disagreeable and repulsive....To those who love God supremely, it is natural to seek amusements, and everything else that we seek, with supreme reference to the glory of God."*[53]

Falling in love with Jesus is the only way to become like Him. *"Jesus divorced Himself from any fulfillment or gratification independent of His Father"* (Katz).[54]

This is sonship, Christ-likeness.

"The secret of an unsatisfied life lies too often in an unsurrendered will" (H. Taylor).[55]

Surrender is the key, not works or determination per se, but a choice to continually surrender and yield unto

God, resulting in love and obedience. Simply, get out of the way of grace and let Him (the Spirit of Grace) be exactly what He is — a teacher who teaches us to say no to ungodliness and grips us with the will and power to do for His good pleasure.

CONCLUSION

We only have one life to live. Don't give your time, energy, and effort into things that are just going to burn.[56] No greater eternal investment exists than giving yourself to God continually. There is nothing greater on this side of eternity than to be a God-filled man.[57] Mother Basilea Schlink wrote in her amazing book, *My All For Him*, "*The dedication of our will leads us into the deepest union of love with Jesus.*"

Smith Wigglesworth spoke of an unquenchable God-craving that actually "*ate away his life.*"[58] John G. Lake said that he felt he was the "*hungriest man (for God) alive.*"[59]

Turn to Him and experience His presence and person. Daily know and crave His voice and nearness. Watch your interest in other things wither away as you are conformed to His image by His nearness. If a cup was full of coffee and it was placed underneath the faucet with crystal clear running water flowing into it, it would only be a matter of time before all the black coffee was rinsed out and only clear water remained. So it is with the spiritual life. Stay under the inflow of God, even if you still feel the residue of black coffee in your soul. Stay under Him and I promise, it is only a matter of time before you are only crystal waters. Make a decision today. I am setting my face towards God. I will sit with Him. I will look to Him. I will shut out other voices and focus on His alone.

This is evidence that there is nothing between you and Him, when you can say, "*To live is Christ....*" What does that mean? *To know Him, to experience Him, and to proclaim Him is all that I live for.* This is the burning thirst. *GOD, RAISE UP AN ARMY OF GOD-CRAVERS!*

"You can't patch up your prayer life when you get to the judgment seat." ~Leonard Ravenhill

"You can delegate many things, but prayer is not one of them." ~A.W. Tozer

"Yesterday's praying will not suffice for today." ~E.M. Bounds

"This period we are in now is a dressing room for eternity, that is all it is." ~Leonard Ravenhill

"In everything, by prayer." ~Philippians 4:6

"Prayer in its highest form is agonizing soul sweat." ~Leonard Ravenhill

"Prayer is the acid test of devotion. Nothing will so stimulate the soul as the honest attempt to pray for others." ~Samuel Chadwick

CHAPTER 5

BURNING INTERCESSOR

"O, that my head were waters and mine eyes a fountain of tears that I might weep day and night...." ~Jeremiah 9:1

The sorrowful truth that such a spiritual employment is largely neglected has negative effects upon more than just our personal standing with God. It dampens what could have otherwise thrived in fire before the Lord. As intercessory prayer remains that which it has always been, we have been *tremendously privileged* to the ear of God having been justified, encouraged, and empowered by His grace to live an obedient life.

The obedient life alone has access to God's ear (Psalm 34:17; Proverbs 15:8; James 4:2,3). Scripture, in no uncertain terms, vastly teaches us the power, significance, and details of a prayer life that God acknowledges. *"All our libraries and studies are mere emptiness compared with our prayer closets"* (C.H. Spurgeon).[60] He who obeys has prayed, and he who would pray, must obey. The importance of prayer was described well by a great man of prayer who said, *"He who puts prayer second puts prayer last."*[61]

THE SPIRIT OF PRAYER

"All our libraries and studies are mere emptiness compared with our prayer closets."[1]
~C.H. Spurgeon

King David overflowed with prayer in the psalms he penned throughout his earthly life, seeing not only its privilege but also its importance by praying morning, noon, and night (Psalm 55:17). He saw the connection between the enlightenment of the Word of God and intimate pleading for the same (Psalm 119:18,19). The Apostle Paul was moved by the same Spirit, encouraging us to pray *"in everything"* (Philippians 4:6). *"In everything"* would entail all our dealings in life: family, money, ministry, study, and the like. This great privilege and importance wasn't something to be active infrequently, but rather *"at all times"* (1 Thessalonians 5:17). *"All times"* encompasses the positive, negative, and mundane. Jesus encouraged us to not only pray, but to endure with persistence, not giving up or *"fainting"* (Luke 18:1). Christ emphasized the importance of prayer by ignoring the potential of its absence in our life. He simply said, *"When you pray"*

(Matthew 6:6). Christ also coupled enduring temptation with prayer (Luke 22:39-46). Scripture reveals to
us the aid in our sufferings is prayer (James 5:13).

THE EFFECTS OF PRAYER

Our aid in worthy living is prayer (2 Thessalonians
1:11). Our aid in wisdom is prayer (James 1:5). Oh,
how our lives would be of such a higher quality if
we lived in persistent, fervent prayer, when trying
situations occur, instead of aimlessly roaming about!
What greater impact would our counsel, words, and
life have upon those weak-hearted Christians who
surround us if our hearts overflowed with burdened,
persistent prayer for them instead of hidden gossip,
jesting, and squandering of time! Let us not take lightly
that he who prays effectually has first lived effectually. In the words of E.M. Bounds, *"He who prays must
obey."*[62] For the wonder of the availability of God's ear
to His people can be blocked by our living! (1 Peter
3:7; Psalm 66:18; 1 John 3:22). The effective prayer of
the righteous man can affect much (James 5:16)! The
availability of God's ear is as glorious of a privilege,
power, and grace as it is a responsibility in our way of
living and use of time.

Christ revealed that prayer for another can keep one
"from the evil one." Prayer can ignite a disciple's life
to be *"separated by the Word"* (John 17:11,15,17,21).
This reveals that merely hearing or reading the Word
will need divine assistance in prayer to affect such a

sanctification of a disciple. As well as the great ability to *"keep"* one *"in His name,"* prayer can affect unity amongst disciples (John 17:11,15,17,21).

Christ, having complete understanding of God's sovereignty, continually imposed upon Himself isolation for the purpose of prayer (Mark 1:35). Do you recall how Christ spent a night in prayer before choosing His twelve disciples (Luke 6:12)? The disciples at Christ's side were interested in learning, not how to teach or heal, but how to pray (Luke 11:2).

THE DISCIPLINE OF PRAYER

"Ignore not the radiant evidence of a praying life."

Once the potential of true prayer is understood, a man can never return, in right heartedness, to a prayerless life. Samuel connected prayerlessness with sin (1 Samuel 12:23). God Himself is seen in Scripture searching for a man to pray (Isaiah 59:16). *"Where is the man who will stir himself to get a hold of God in prayer?"* (Isaiah 64:7). *"Oh, for determined men and women, who will rise early and really burn out for God"* (Hodge).[63] True prayer is not a light matter. Nor is it an exercise for the slothful. Christ Himself offered up prayers with *"loud crying and tears"* (Hebrews 5:7). He burned in agony and fervency in Gethsemane (Luke 22:14). Christ taught us that prayer isn't a weak-hearted matter, nor is it an exercise for lazy knees. For the key to its effectiveness is importunity (Luke 11:5-13). Hezekiah's prayers moved God to add fifteen years upon his life (Isaiah 38:1-5). God hears. God listens, to the righteous (James 5:16; Psalm 66:18). He who has the ear of God, and sincerely applies himself to such a divine employment, has access to a fruitful ministry. The writer of Hebrews asked for prayer (Hebrews 13:18). Paul asked for such a divine assistance to be added

"A burden is a revelation of a tremendous spiritual need, able to be satisfied by God alone, having no avenue where by it can be expressed, save, groaning which cannot be uttered...."

to his ministry (2 Thessalonians 3:1). Charles Spurgeon has a famous article pleading for the prayers of the saints on the behalf of ministers entitled, "Brethren, Pray For Us." Paul knew the power of true prayer could turn events in the spreading of the Word of God (Philippians 1:19). What called down an angel to release Peter out of jail? It was not power, but prayer.

Paul recorded that the aid to his ministry was none other than true prayer (2 Corinthians 1:11). Prayer can open doors for uttering the Word of God (Colossians 4:3-4). What a responsibility, that will, without question, be one of many things we give an account for before the judgment seat!

THE WORD AND PRAYER

The recorded lesson from the apostolic Church was that dedication of one's self should be given to the Word of God, but equally to prayer (Acts 6:4). Just as Elijah, in the Old Testament, prayed for eyes to be opened to see, Paul prayed for the enlightening of the eyes of our heart that we may see (2 Kings 6:17; Ephesians 1:19).

Ignore not the radiant evidence of a praying life. It may well open and enlighten a man's heart to see what he couldn't by study alone. The hope of His coming Kingdom is revealed in the Scriptures as the anchor of our soul (Hebrews 6:19). Faith is the currency of the Kingdom (Hebrews 11:6). Love is the character of the Kingdom (Galatians 5). These must be the center of our life if we are to live a life pleasing to the Lord (Hebrews 11:6; 10:39). We, dull of hearing, slow of heart, we need the spirit of prayer to quicken us with grace to walk out that which is currently in our mouths (Colossians 1:9-11; Ephesians 1:16-19; 3:14-20).

The great protection to prayerless praying (a disease rampant amongst the carnal) is first of all absolute surrender, sincerity, and the honest, humble dependence upon His Spirit to reveal His Word to us, for nothing else is a lamp unto our feet as we tread down the dark path of a deceptive world and religion (Psalm 119:105). Paul prayed according to God's working (Ephesians 1:19; 3:20). Christ eclipsed His will with God's (Matthew 26:39).

"Prayerless praying, how popular! Yet, useless" (E.M. Bounds).[64] The Pharisees prayed to be heard, seen, and recognized, with many words and a prideful disposition, to be honored for the good they had done

(Mark 6:5; Luke 18:10-14). Leonard Ravenhill said, *"The secret of prayer is praying in secret"* (Matthew 6:6).[65] As the culmination of man's day draws to a close, the sobriety of the Church's secret place will be the Church's secret to victory (1 Peter 4:7). We must soberly strive in prayer and allow the Spirit of God to move us in intercession so as to sweeten the bitter areas of our lives, and the lives of those that God has given us, knowing, at times only the Spirit will know the will of God (Romans 15:30-31; 8:8-26).

BURDENED PRAYER

A burden is a revelation of a tremendous spiritual need, able to be satisfied by God alone, having no avenue whereby it can be expressed, save, groaning which cannot be uttered, explained, or understood.

"Prayers that cannot be uttered are often prayers that cannot be refused" (Spurgeon).[66]

Leonard Ravenhill challenges,

> *"No man is greater than his prayer life...
> let me live with a man awhile and share his
> prayer life, and then I will tell you how tall
> I think he is or how majestic I think he is in
> God....You may impress others but you can't
> impress God. You can show off on the plat-
> form, singing, preaching, and doing your
> stuff, but not in prayer....Praying men stop
> sinning, and sinning men stop praying.*

Can he share His sorrow with you? Can you remember the last time you couldn't go to bed because men were dying without Christ? When was the last time you pushed the plate away and said, 'No, I need more time with God'? God looks for a man, not a seraphim, not a cherubim, not a half man and half deity. God looks for men, not money, not methods, not machinery, not movements...Men! We need to say, 'Lord, I'm concerned, I am speeding up to eternity; look at my ministry, look at the secrets of my life, look at my fruit-lessness, look at my dry eyes, look at my poor spirit that has no ache in it, look at me!'"[67]

"The great day of accountability alone will reveal all that could have been affected through a selfless management of your time to invest in prayer."

The great day of accountability alone will reveal all that could have been affected through a selfless management of our time to invest in prayer. Beware to stand not ashamed. You cannot return to live the way you should have. Dr. Michael L. Brown urged us, *"Are you spending your time, energy, and efforts on things that are just going to burn?"*[68] The investment of time in prayer for others yields eternal rewards as it effects this temporal situation with everlasting effects. I tell you, after a diligent study of God's Word, you will find this common thread: an obedient life lived in humble intercession avails greatly in the eyes of God. A.W. Tozer, at the end of his life, said this challenging statement, *"I don't think that I will be ashamed of the things that I have done in my life, but rather what I could have done."*[69] Samuel Chadwick, at the end of his life, said this sobering statement, *"I have spent two-thirds of my life in Bible study and one-third of my life in prayer. If I had the chance to do it all over again, I would spend two-thirds of my life in prayer and one-third of my life in Bible study."*[70] The Word of God should never be neglected or despised (thought little of), for without its direction, one will more often than not, spend his time amiss. Prayer and the Scriptures together constitute the whole of God's assistance toward us.

PRAYER AND THE JUDGMENT SEAT

Let us sincerely ask ourselves, in the light of Him who sees through the outward actions and into the motives and intents (Revelation 2:23; Hebrews 4:12), what does it matter if we boldly dance in the assembly, pray with eloquence and volume, shamelessly raise our hands amongst others, or even speak the depths of the Scriptures if we are bankrupt before God in the quiet place? *"The true test of a man's soul is when he is alone"* (Jeremy Taylor).[71] Have you come to the face of others from the face of God (figuratively)? To truly know God is to truly share, in our small degree, His feelings, revealed to us in His Word, experienced by us in prayer. To share not God's burden is to share not in His heart, and He who is most dear to God is he who lays his head upon His breast (John 13:23, 25). There is pain in God's heart for humanity. And only that man whom God has been able to draw to Himself in intimacy will know it, share it, and take it upon himself to labor together in an attempt to ease the pain of God's broken heart.[72]

"Nothing will so test and stimulate the Christian life as the honest attempt to pray for others" (Andrew Murray).[73] *"The men who have done mighty things for God have always been mighty in prayer, have well understood the possibilities of prayer, and have made the most of these opportunities.... Men who know how to pray are the greatest boon God can give the earth – they are the richest gift earth can offer heaven"* (E.M. Bounds).[74]

"A disciple who will give himself to the divine work of pure ministry of the Word and prayer for others will affect greatly the course and pattern of living of these to whom he ministers" (Colossians 4:12).

A disciple who will give himself to the divine preparation and work of a constant receiving and obeying God's Word, soaked in personal and intercessory prayer, will be more confident at the Judgment, knowing that he not only fed his spirit with the truth of God's Word, but he also opened his spirit to share God's heart. A disciple who will give himself to the divine work of pure ministry of the Word and prayer for others will affect greatly the course and pattern of living of these to whom he ministers (Colossians 4:12).

Of what greater significance can prayer be than that ministry which makes effective all else? The reward for a correct, sincere, and fervent life of prayer will more so than all others, be most significant in that great day. *"There is no alternative to prayer and obedience"* (Ravenhill).[75] *"For it is a great honor to speak to men on behalf of God, but an even greater honor to speak to God on behalf of men"* (E.M. Bounds).[76]

Let us not know the guilt and shame of a life that chose to avoid the *power, importance, privilege,* and *responsibility* of the availability of God's ear. Let us not forget that even He who was the Word made flesh lived a life of fervent prayer. Let us plead for divine assistance for ourselves, and others, as we pursue the approval of God (2 Corinthians 5:9; James 1:12; 1 Corinthians 9:27) through conformity to the image of God's Son through nothing other than interaction with His Spirit!

"It is the duty of every Christian to be Christ to his neighbor." ~Martin Luther

"The only problem with scheduled outreaches is that if you can turn it on, you can turn it off." ~Bill Johnson

"If your Gospel isn't touching others, it hasn't touched you!" ~Curry R. Blake

"How you believe God perceives people will determine how you respond to them." ~Jacquelyn K. Heasley

"Sympathy is no substitute for action."
~David Livingstone

"'Not called!' did you say? 'Not heard the call,' I think you should say. Put your ear down to the Bible, and hear Him bid you go and pull sinners out of the fire of sin. Put your ear down to the burdened, agonized heart of humanity, and listen to its pitiful wail for help. Go stand by the gates of hell, and hear the damned entreat you to go to their father's house and bid their brothers and sisters and servants and masters not to come there. Then look Christ in the face – whose mercy you have professed to obey – and tell Him whether you will join heart and soul and body and circumstances in the march to publish His mercy to the world." ~William Booth

"The world out there is not waiting for a new definition of Christianity but a new demonstration."
~Leonard Ravenhill

CHAPTER 6

BURNING GOSPEL

"My message and my preaching were not with wise and persuasive words, but with a demonstration of the Spirit's power, so that your faith might not rest on men's wisdom, but on God's power."
~1 Corinthians 2:4-5

Demonstration: *"The action of showing the existence or truth of something by giving proof or evidence."*[77]

The Gospel is not a verbal argument for the existence of God. It is above all things, the demonstration of God's love and a demonstration of God's power. It is the evidence of who He is, in His love, by the reality of His broken body on the cursed cross and the supernatural power that breaks into the earth through that same cross.

I remember a close friend of mine who traveled with Reinhard Bonnke for a number of years told me a story. When Evangelist Bonnke was labeled a *"healing evangelist,"* he responded, *"A healing evangelist is the only kind of evangelist that there is in the Bible. The evangelists that don't heal are a recent development."* Bill Johnson said, *"Jesus did miracles because it was necessary to reveal the Father. He gives us miracles to teach us how to see."*[78] The reason is simple; we don't want the faith of individuals to rest on the cleverness or wisdom of arguments, but on the demonstration of God's love and power. His love and His power are His cross, both of which are the Gospel in the person of Jesus Christ.

We must seek to embody these things in our daily lives. *"For I am not ashamed of the Gospel, for it is the **power of God"** (Romans 1:16). We, as the Church, need to ask ourselves, what gospel are we giving? As it is commonly known, the word "gospel" means *"good news."* What *"good news"* was given to you? Was it the power of God? Was it alive by the influence of the supernatural reality of God in the Spirit, or was it just words that mentally persuaded you? The Scriptures tell us that the Gospel isn't a matter of clever speech but of *"demonstration of the Spirit and power"* (1 Corinthians 2:4). And in the letter to the Thessalonians, Paul says that the Gospel comes in *"...conviction,"* which is not an ounce less supernatural.

There is a reason for this.

*"**So that,** your faith would not rest upon the **wisdom of men** but **on the power of God"** (1 Corinthians 2:5).

This shows us that some people's faith can rest and does rest upon the wisdom of men. What does this mean? Some people believe because it was cleverly explained to them. And, after they weighed out the religious options and benefits, they chose Christianity. People search for a religion and when they find whichever one seems right in their eyes, "sign up" and change their lives accordingly. They live somewhat happily, having satisfied their religious itch. But they fail to realize that Christianity is not a change of life, but an exchange of life.

Faith that rests on man's wisdom and cleverness does not and never will lead to a life that actually possesses resurrection power. It is the mere following of religious teachings, systems of forgiveness and rules, while professing hope in an afterlife, all of which most religions emphasize.

When you have received the Gospel as the power of God in your life, then you really have life in Him. *"He who has the Son has life"* (1 John 5:12). It is undeniable. Your devotion is not a matter of keeping up with your deci-

"The real Christian reality is that a higher quality of existence has entered into you and you now have a hatred for sin and a real love for Jesus inside of you."

sion to live a changed life by doing your best to follow Christian teachings. The real Christian reality is that a higher quality of existence has entered into you and you now have a hatred for sin and a real love for Jesus inside of you.

The Gospel **is** the *"power of God."* It is not "like" the power of God. It is not "the way to" the power of God. *"It is the power of God."*

JESUS IS THE GOSPEL

How can a message be the *"power of God"*? The message is the power of God simply because the message is a Man. Jesus Christ is the Gospel of God. The Gospel is not merely a history lesson about Jesus Christ; it *is* Jesus Christ (Hebrews 1:1). He is the Word of God (John 1:1,14). He is the message of God to the world. The good news of Jesus Christ is that deliverance and power, forgiveness and peace, hope and love, are found in a person, not a thinking pattern. God didn't send Jesus to die to get everyone to sign up on His team. He sent Jesus to die in order to bring mankind into Himself and restore mankind from the fall, work through mankind in the earth, and in the end, set mankind on high to reign with Christ in the age to come.

"Salvation only comes by the power of God, who is Christ, God's speaking, coming into you through the door of faith, or more easily understood, your surrender to Him."

Notice that the apostles didn't preach about Christ. They preached Christ Himself (Acts 5:42; 17:3; 2 Corinthians 4:5). As T. Austin Sparks noted, *"God speaks Himself."*[79] This is how men are born again. They couldn't possibly be born from above by a nominal belief system or by adherence to correct thinking patterns. Doctrine has never saved a person. Salvation only comes by the power of God, who is Christ, God's speaking, coming into you through the door of faith, or more easily understood, your surrender to Him. Paul told Titus that God *"manifested His Word (Jesus) through preaching..."* (Titus 1:3). The Gospel is the manifestation of Christ. It is in this manifestation of Christ that men meet Him. For God, who said, *"Let light shine out of darkness, made His light shine in our hearts to give us the Light of the knowledge of the glory of God in the **face of Christ**"* (2 Corinthians 4:6).

Christ is the light (John 8:12), giving us a relationship with God by divine enlightenment.

Christ is the life (John 14:6), giving us an eternal quality of existence.

Christ is the way (John 14:6), revealing not only the route to the Father, but also the way of life for those born of the Spirit.

Christ is the truth (John 14:6), the perfect wholeness of life and existence.

To truly preach Christ is to bring men into contact with the person of Jesus Christ! It is the reconciliation of God and man. It is impossible to meet Him without fatal damage to your old life. He is power! Freedom is in a Man named Jesus—not a belief system, religion, or an attempt to make a life change. The Gospel is the power of God, for it is the meeting of man and God, in

Jesus Christ, to all who will cast themselves upon Him in absolute (which is to say genuine) faith.

LOVE IN POWER

Love is the greatest demonstration of power that there is; in Christ's love He became a man and went to the cross, and through His death He destroyed the power of the enemy.

Power is the undeniable demonstration of God's love. We have seen men on the streets who have little to no belief in God, encounter Jesus when their torn ACL was completely and supernaturally mended before their eyes. In that moment, there is nothing that a man can do other than ask, *"How did that just happen?"* For they had done nothing to earn the privilege of being supernaturally healed, but His loving care for them was extended to them even in their rebellion and ignorance.

"Love still holds the key to His power, and His power showcases His love."

Love still holds the key to His power, and His power showcases His love; love and power embody the testimony and the demonstration of the Gospel in the person of Jesus Christ.

LOVE

"Do everything in love" (1 Corinthians 16:14). We ought to have no agenda but to love people. God's agenda has always been to love mankind. His reaching out to

humanity, which reached its climax in the crushing of His Son, is the love message. First Corinthians 13:1-8 states, *"Without love we are nothing, love never fails."* Let us drop all other agendas and expectations we may have in order to be free to simply, selflessly, love people by introducing them to the person of Jesus Christ. It seems we are bound by our agendas and drained by our expectations, but love is freedom, for it is not something to do, but to be. Let us focus on the perfect love of God and let love melt the hearts of men. Even if they don't receive the Gospel that day, they will never be able to shake off the fact that we loved them enough to tell them of His irresistible love and the truth of their worthless state apart from Him.

The other day I was in McDonalds. In striking up a conversation with some young guys, I was able to give them the Gospel and present to them the opportunity to get right with God through Jesus'

"So how empty is the testimony of God's love, if it is void of love itself?"

work on their behalf. The major hang-up was a common one. They said, *"I know that I will not stop living the way that I am living."* I proceeded to tell them that we don't clean ourselves up to come to God, but we come to God and He cleans us up. It was to no avail. They continued on about their sexual addictions and adultery. When I saw it was getting nowhere due to their inoculation to the Gospel through religion, I asked them if they had any pain in their bodies. One guy had destroyed his back in a car accident a few years prior and had chronic pain ever since. I asked him, *"Do you have pain in it right now?"* He replied, *"YES!"* Knowing how important that moment was, and how much God loves to demonstrate Himself, even to religious, rebellious wretches, I reached out and put my hand on his back. He immediately broke out in tears and his face turned blood red. Power shot into his back and he was healed. He said, *"What just went straight through me? I am hot all over."* I began to tell him about hell, refreshing his memory that, *"a loving Savior will one day be a severe judge."*[80] I also told him that if he didn't drink the cup of God's mercy now, he would be forced to drink of the cup of His wrath later. I informed him that it was God's love that was convicting him of sin and it would give him a free way out through the surrender of repentance. Though he didn't allow us to pray with him to surrender to Jesus, I know that he will never forget that encounter with God's full love he had that day in McDonalds. So we love. Fully love. Full love shows both sides of God's mercy and manifests His power. *"The cross shows us simultaneously how much God hates sin and how much He loves the sinner."*[81]

EXTENDING HIS LOVE

"Jesus did not come to shame sinners but to save them."[82] Evangelism is spreading the good news — Jesus — offering men freedom from sin, which is the greatest expression of love. So how empty is the testimony of God's love, if it is void of love itself? Love's presence during evangelism shows that we not only believe

what we are saying, but also care that men are literally walking toward an eternal fire. God's Word says, "*The fruit of the Spirit is love*" (Galatians 5), and, "*For the love of God is shed abroad in our hearts by the Holy Spirit*" (Romans 5:5); therefore, the result of the Holy Spirit's work in our lives will be love. Love cares for others, especially their eternal standing in relationship with God. We should never forget that God makes men like Jesus, and Jesus laid His life down for others. What a delusion a man is in if his "spirituality" is loveless, so as to live a life of numbness to a lost and dying world. K.P. Yohannan said, "*Years ago I came to a crisis in my life. I realized that if hell was real, I must do something more than what I was doing with my life.*"[83]

FEARLESS PREACHING

Love is best defined as "selflessness," since, "*Greater love has no man than this, that he would lay down his life for his friends*" (John 15:13). This is why "*Perfect love casts out all fear*" (1 John). Fear is based out of self-consciousness and self-preservation, while love is being conscious of others before us. We are slaves to fear, to the degree that we love our lives, and to the degree that we love our lives, we will fail to be witnesses; we will simply be restrained by fear and self-interest from the love that makes us true witnesses. Our Christianity is silent to the degree that we love ourselves. Oh frozen silent Christian, you have accepted a false spirituality! But if we will allow the Holy Spirit to be a constant presence in our lives, His love will expand in our hearts and self-consciousness will burn away and our lives will become second to His purposes and plan. In loving not our lives by true love, God will be free to extend His hand to the world through us. Love is the goal. Love is the incentive. Love is the inspiration. Love is the power. Love is the Gospel. Love never fails.

POWER

"When God made it possible for the Spirit that raised Jesus Christ from the dead to live in you and me, He made powerlessness inexcusable....[85] Jesus did not leave us powerless. He never desired us to go without power. To do God's work we need God's power. There is no witness without power. A good news without power is not good."[84]
~Bill Johnson

The power of the Holy Spirit is for the preaching of the Gospel (Isaiah 61:1). Witnesses are those who have the power of the Holy Spirit upon their lives (Acts 1:8). The power of the Spirit is for the delivering of the captives (Acts 10:38). Paul shows us that he was not ashamed of the Gospel, because it is the power of God. Many people are ashamed of the Gospel because they have never seen it as the power of God. To see the Gospel as the power of God will destroy this shame. It will place confidence in the right place by removing it from who we can become and emphasize what Christ has done.

A demonstration of power forces a decision by those who witness it, because it shows God to the individual in an undeniable way. We see the sick healed on the streets, and it is such an arresting moment in the individual's life. Even in their shock, they are stuck with the evidence that God has just touched them. Even if they are not sick, we seek to pray for them in an attempt to usher the presence of God into their hearts. As they sense Him, who is the desire of the nations, they break internally. Power is irreplaceable.

Without power we can end up as phony as the door-to-door salesman whose product does not work when he is asked for a demonstration.[86] Power is God coming into the lives of men. Power is love. Power is the Gospel. Power is the demonstrated presence of God. Not only have we seen cancer, hepatitis, broken arms or wrists, strained backs, sprained ankles, vision, ribs, and much more healed, but sometimes just the look on our faces as we genuinely care for people through the love of Christ breaks the hearts of people. I believe the face of the Gospel is in the face of the one whose face is staring at Christ's face.

I remember a story by David Hogan, a missionary to the jungles of Mexico. He came to pray for a woman with legs that were twisted backwards by demonic power through a witch doctor. He walked in the room and said to her, "*The Kingdom of God is here*," to which she replied, "*Where is it?*" He raised his hands in the air so as to draw all her attention to himself and said,

"You're looking at it." I love that! We must see that Christ in us is greater than any force in the world.

WE CAN'T STOP SPEAKING

In Acts chapter 4 we see the disciples standing on trial. They are commanded to stop preaching Jesus. Look at part of their response. They said, *"We can't stop speaking about what we have seen and heard."* There seems to be the reverse effect in the American church today, because we can't start speaking (for the most part). The reason that there is a divide between the apostles, *who couldn't stop speaking*, and the modern American church, *who can't start speaking*, is because the issue of speaking lies in the issue of seeing and hearing. Jesus said, *"What you have heard in the dark, speak in the light."*

Many modern American Christians aren't hearing the voice of God in their lives, and very rarely see anything in God. Their spiritual eyes are darkened and because of this, they have nothing living inside of them to speak out. Not only that, but because they don't speak out, they don't see anything happen that would build their faith. As Bill Johnson noted, *"The first step to growing in miracles is to pray for the sick."*[87]

I believe that if we really spent quality time in His presence, consistently depending on Him for life, our ears would pop open. I believe here, in the place of hearing, our eyes would be unveiled to see. And, having seen and heard from the Lord, we would have a bursting spring of the love of God inside of us for a lost and dying world. We would be leaking deliverance to our surroundings. It is my conviction that the life of Sonship is inflow, overflow, and outflow. The outflow is the result of an overflow, which is a result of a great inflow. God will touch those around you to the degree you touch God or He has touched you.

Brother, if you have an issue getting yourself to speak, take care of the root issue and go get with Jesus. Let Him show you His heart and place it inside of you. I promise, like the apostles of old, you will have a hard time passing people on the street because you are burning to tell them of His wonderful love for them simply because it is really real to you. If there is still a film of fear over your mouth, you must see that whatever you give attention to will grow. If you give attention to faith, it will grow. But if you give attention to doubt, it will grow. Ignore doubt and go in faith.

TESTIMONIES

Salvation and healing on the street – While walking around a park, my friend and I saw a man sitting on a bench by himself. We figured that he was waiting for us. So we brought the Gospel to him. Not only did he give his life to Jesus as we told him of the

"So the wounds of our Savior cried out to us on his behalf."

wonderful Savior who didn't come to shame sinners but to save them, but he also told us that he had a torn cartilage in his knee and he was in a lot of pain. And because of this, he couldn't work. So the wounds of our Savior cried out to us on his behalf. As we prayed for him, all his pain left his knee by a supernatural mending. Also, a word of knowledge about his religious past broke his heart and his eyes filled with tears as the presence of God came upon him in power and love.

Homosexual set free in jail – We also go into the local jail every week to bring the power of the Gospel to those hurting lives. We have seen many miracles as well as hundreds bow their hearts to Jesus with tears of repentance. We do not preach against homosexuality; we preach Jesus. But I had a man come to me after a few weeks of preaching Jesus in the jail and he said, *"I know that I am delivered from homosexuality. I feel completely different and the spirit of perversion is gone."* We don't preach against drugs; we preach Jesus. But I had a guy come to me who has been out of jail for a few months and say, *"I haven't touched drugs and I have no desire to."*

Broken wrist healed – One of my favorite testimonies of the power of the Gospel was when I met a man who had a cast on his arm. He had been clipped under his legs during a basketball game and fell on his wrist and fractured it in two places. Before I began to preach the Gospel, I noticed him. I called him up in front all his fellow peers, and all those curious eyes watched God touch his wrist. After feeling heat shoot into his wrist, the man removed the cast and began to laugh, as it was completely restored. The place erupted with praise; his wrist was fused back together instantly. We have watched the power of the Gospel destroy the effects of sin and sickness. This Gospel is simple. Believe it. Proclaim it. Trust Jesus to back it with His power. He will, if you do not grow weary in your pursuit of Him.

Hepatitis healed – In jail a few months back, I met a young man named Kris. He responded to an altar call to surrender to Jesus. Shortly after that I saw him in tears as the Holy Spirit began to move on him during a time of ministry. He explained to me that he had hepatitis for along time, and was on medication and could not gain any weight. After we prayed for him, I didn't see him for a while and I realized that he had been released to go home. He ended up contacting me to work with us on the streets and to tell me that he had stopped taking his medication and he had gained a lot of weight because he was healed of hepatitis.

Cancer healed at a bus stop – On a Tuesday street outreach, we ran into a man waiting at a bus stop. He was waiting for the bus to take him to his prostate cancer checkup. We knew he was really waiting for us—not the bus. So we told him of God's healing power and gave him the Gospel. Not only did he pray with us, but he also promised that if he was healed, he would come to our local church and testify about his healing. Needless to say, he came to the local church that Sunday and testified that they couldn't find the cancer in his prostate anymore.

Ankle healed in the mall – I was in the mall and saw a young man with crutches. Crutches, hearing aids, and wheelchairs are all green lights to bring the Kingdom of God to that needy person. So I ran over to him. He was confused as to why I ran over to him. As I asked what happen to his foot, he proceeded to tell me that he sprained his ankle really bad and he couldn't put pressure on it. He tried to move away from me, but I persisted, "Do you mind if I pray for it?" He said, "What?" I asked him again and he said, "Go ahead, if you want to." God touched his ankle as I got down on my knees and prayed, with passing peers and families slowing down to see what I was doing to this other man's foot in the middle of the mall by a Sprint store. He was in shock that God would touch him. He was a little afraid of the power and wanted to get away from us. We pressed the Gospel on his heart as he picked up his crutches and walked away with an undeniable healing of his ankle.

Healing of passing janitor – Another moving testimony was when I got out of an elevator and I saw a janitor limping while pushing a cart of cleaning supplies. I stopped him and asked why he was limping. He proceeded to tell me how many years ago he had an accident and ruined his knee for life. I asked him if it was painful and he replied, "Very much so." So I asked him if he knew Jesus and he said he did, so I went ahead and knelt down right there and grabbed his knee. It was only three seconds later that he was visibly moved because his knee was instantly healed.

Chest cancer vanished – A man came to the altar with a painful cancer lump on his chest. It was difficult for him to breath. It was difficult for him to lie down. It was growing and spreading. When we laid our hands on him and commanded the cancer to die in the name of Jesus, he began to weep. The lump did not disappear right there. But his heart was touch by the presence of the Holy Spirit. I came back to the same place to minister again a few weeks later and he came up with tears in his eyes, saying that the lump was gone and he had many others feel for it in his chest so that he wasn't dreaming. Later that week he went to the doctor for X-rays. The current X-rays were placed next to the old X-rays, and it was the site of a miracle to see that the current X-rays had no trace of cancer. Jesus is alive!

Healing of a door-to-door salesman – This next one is fun. I was praying in my room, home alone, and the doorbell rang. I was frustrated because I wanted to be alone for the day with God. But I felt I should attend to the door. I opened the door only to see a salesman seeking to get me a new windshield for my car. As I listened to him, I turned my heart within to hear what the Holy Spirit had to say about this guy. I didn't hear anything for about twenty minutes. So, I just let the man talk and I worshipped Jesus internally. Then just before I turned to leave, I instantly knew he had pain in his legs. I asked about it and he said, "I walk from house to house every day and I have really bad shin issues. They hurt always." I asked him if he believed in Jesus and he said, "No. But I think He was a good guy." I gave him the Gospel again and I knelt down on the ground outside my house and said, "In Jesus' name, shins be made whole to testify of the love of Jesus to this unbeliever." Instantly he became hot and his pain was gone. He was in shock at the fact that a God he didn't even believe in touched his personal pain that he dealt with every day. What a loving God! That salesman will never forget that day.

"If you pray for 100 people that have not been healed, you must pray for person 101 as if all 100 before him were healed."

~Reinhard Bonnke

If you have been praying for the sick and seeing very little results, let me encourage you with something that Reinhard Bonnke said to me when I asked him about praying for the sick. He said, *"If you pray for 100 people that have not been healed, you must pray for person 101 as if all 100 before him were healed."* Healing is a demonstration of the Gospel to point people to Jesus. But the greatest miracle of all is when God *"takes an unholy man out of an unholy world, makes him holy, and then places him back into that unholy world and keeps him holy"* (Leonard Ravenhill). We must demonstrate the Gospel in order to introduce men to Jesus, because, only if they meet Jesus will they be reconciled to God.

I could compile a whole book of similar testimonies of God's amazing Gospel power. I share them with you to build your faith in the finished work of Christ. Let us set our hearts on understanding what He has done, more than on what we can become. When Jesus said, *"It is finished,"* what He was saying was, *"I just put an end to everything that Adam set in motion."*

Let us get alone with Jesus. He will speak and show us Himself. God will form the yielded life into the image of the Son of God who lays His life down for others and displays God's nature in the world. This is the divine inflow of God that causes an outflow of God! As Reinhard Bonnke said, *"You must hear the word, 'Come,' before the word, 'GO.'"*

"Unless we have invested a great deal of time in our secret ministry to the Lord, then the shallowness of our public ministry will be very evident. Today it is abundantly clear that not enough time is spent ministering to the Lord, and way too much time is spent ministering to people; hence, most of what is done in the name of ministry is performed in a fleshly, human way which never bears any lasting fruit." ~Chip Brogden

PRESENTING THE FULLNESS OF THE GOSPEL

We must understand that if there was a way for Jesus to be Savior and not Lord, than "salvation" would never deal with the root issues in Eden (man's rebellion). The submission to the reign of Christ in the human soul is the teeth of the Gospel; the Lordship of Jesus demands the surrender to His rule. Jesus didn't come to give men forgiveness alone. Who doesn't want forgiveness? We could "save the world" just offering forgiveness. He came to reconcile men to God. Reconciliation is only a reality in submission to His rule.

For the most part, America has preached a partial Gospel; because we are afraid to puncture people, we take the teeth out of the Gospel. We must understand that to remove the teeth of the Gospel is to remove the good news from the good news. A lady said to me the other day, *"God doesn't convict people to give their lives to Him in order to save them; He shows them His goodness, then they give their lives to Him."* To which I replied, *"Conviction is His goodness."* He is so good to convict us. He is so good to take the management of our lives away from us. The man who wants to manage his own life knowing that God desires to manage it is full of selfish ambition and pride, all of which must be laid at the feet of Christ. Because, without conviction there can be no repentance, and what is repentance if we maintain the ruling of our own lives? Our identification with Christ's cross is through surrendering our hands to be nailed with His.

"To be convicted is to be brought to the place where we can actually lay our lives down at the feet of Jesus."

Conviction is a gift straight from the good heart of God. The lack of delivering the fullness of the Gospel brings men all the way to the door but refuses to tell them how to turn the handle. We cannot fall into the trap of preaching the power of the Kingdom of God without repentance, nor fall into the trap of preaching repentance without the power of the Kingdom. To be convicted is to be brought to the place where we can actually lay our lives down at the feet of Jesus. Without conviction man only acknowledges Jesus. But to believe in response to an internal Spirit conviction is not partial or conditional. To surrender to this Kingdom is not withholding. Faith in its very essence of meaning is contrary to partiality. Paul explains to us in Galatians that any alteration by addition to the Gospel will severe us from Christ. *"A diluted Gospel is no Gospel at all"* (David Wilkerson).

One of the most impacting statements on this subject is from Art Katz when he said, *"The idolatrous religions are those that give men a small measure of religious satisfaction yet, they allow men to retain the lordship of their own lives."*[88]

It dawned on me one day that if the devil can seduce Christianity away from the cross, he will create the most successfully "positive" — death trap that there has ever been. Paul warned about *"another Jesus"* (1 Corinthians 11:4) and a Jesus that isn't King, isn't Jesus. A Jesus that doesn't remove you from being the manager of your own life is not King Jesus. The greatest news in the world is that God will take your wicked-sinful-no-good management of your life and will resurrect it, giving you divine purity, power, and life. Death for life is the main principle of the Kingdom. Everything in God is gained by death. God has no obsession with death. He loves resurrection life! He can only resurrect that which is dead. Needless to say, any "gospel" that allows you to retain the lordship of your own life is no good news at all. It is not Jesus, but a manipulation of things through a message about "Jesus." It doesn't save, because it fails to enter into the reality of what salvation is.

CONCLUSION

In summary, the Gospel is a demand to release your life into the hands of God so that He can clean it and make it new. In burning with the Gospel, let us give the fullness of the Gospel. God doesn't just want to forgive and heal, but to reign. In fact, in order for Him to forgive, He must reign; and just because He healed doesn't mean He forgave or reigns in the life. If He forgave and didn't reign, there would never be a new creation. His rule is marching forward in which is His pardon. We proclaim the Kingdom of God in all of its powerful effects of healing, deliverance from devils, miracles, forgiveness, and power over sin, all wrought by the blood of Jesus so that men may partake of the resurrection life of Christ urging men to repent by turning from sin to God. We are His delivering agents in the world. Go into Walmart, the mall, your campus, your work, in the power of the Spirit, to bring the fullness of the benefits purchased by the cross—realized by us in intimacy—and demand repentance from self and faith towards God, to a hurting, dying world, that they may meet Jesus in His full goodness and be prepared for His return.

Let us fight the devil where he is and with the only weapon that can defeat his oppressions, sickness, sin, and bondage. He dwells in the spirit (Ephesians 6:12) and the only weapon able to destroy his power is the Gospel of the cross of Christ (Hebrews 2:14). It would be ridiculous to be standing in your kitchen trying to box a man on the front porch. It is my opinion that we must strike the root of the issues in mankind with the name of Jesus in the power of the Gospel instead of trying to bring some type of moral change or intellectual factual argument. Let me end this chapter on the burning Gospel with this quote from a book by Andrew Murray on the state of the Church.

"There are four different planes of power – the lowest is the physical, above that is the mental, above that is the moral, and above all is the spiritual. It is only when a man moves on the spiritual level that he has power with God.

It is because too many ministers and Christian workers are content to live upon the intellectual level or upon the moral plane, that their work is impotent to touch the mighty stronghold of Satan.

The first question, therefore, to put to every Christian worker is: on what level are you working; on what level are you living? For if you are speaking on anything less than the Spirit level, you should know that your life will be largely a failure."[89]

~F.B. Meyer (Quoted in Andrew Murray's book, The State of the Church, An Urgent Call to Repentance and Prayer, page 41.)

—ᘍᐤᘍ—

"The Church cannot be properly defined; it must be demonstrated." ~Dr. Robert Gladstone

"There is nothing that makes us love a man so much as praying for him." ~William Law

"The end-time demands upon the Church will require a community situation...the Church is to perfect our wisdom and knowledge on how to live with each other." ~Art Katz

"...love one another." ~JESUS

"...how good and pleasant it is for brethren to dwell together in unity." ~Psalm 133

"The Church is a race and not a place; a people and not a steeple. Church isn't somewhere we go, but what we are. All doing should issue out of our being." ~Unknown

—ᘍᐤᘍ—

CHAPTER 7

BURNING TOGETHER

"And the glory which thou hast given me I have given unto them; that they may be one, even as we are one."
~John 17:22

The cultivation of a community situation is crucial for the growth of any individual's spiritual life. The safety net of deeply spiritual relationships and honest love for one another is essential. God, in His glorious wisdom, has fashioned it so. In Ephesians, Paul speaks about *"speaking the truth in love"* as the way to maturity (Ephesians 4:15). We need that wondrous medium of communication flowing through each other to each other. It is common knowledge that all friendships in this life are built upon communication, but we, who are born again by the Spirit, possess speech of another kind. We possess divine interaction and exchange from each individual's specific unique color in which Christ proceeds. Though such spiritual realities are so rare amongst brothers today, I have had the privilege of sharing in some precious times of such divine exchange. I have also made it a part of my daily life. Such a resolve, I believe, is in line with Christ's seemingly idyllic desire to make all of His own, one.

"Burning deep in the heart of God for His Church is a desire for bonding—fastening into oneness." Spiritual union by love in Christ is a feeling that nothing can describe. It is best seen as, *"light,"* or *"life,"* or *"love,"* in a manner only naturally likened to that of the early flawless friendships of adolescent years. Short as this falls to authentic communion by the Spirit with one another, I have nothing natural with which to describe it adequately. Such fellowship is experienced in only one arena. It is the honest, open-faced, "eyeball to eyeball" transparency of a selfless kind that looks past the human suit and person, into the residence of God in that man who stands before you. For this, there is no natural equal. There is no greater protection from the blindsided seductions of the evil one then such open speaking soaked in selflessness.

LOVE UNITY

"Love is the perfect bond of unity" (Colossians 3:14), and our unity is to be *"of the Spirit in the bond of peace"* (Ephesians 4:3). Robert Gladstone used to say, *"There is*

a difference between speaking spiritual and speaking in the Spirit."[90] The connection of such a spiritual kind is a "*bond*" or an actual "*fastening together.*" Burning deep in the heart of God for His Church is a desire for a spiritual bonding—fastening into one-

"...community is a people of common union, sharing spiritual communion, keeping a common unity. "

ness; moving together, fitly joined, and completing one another (Ephesians 4:16). Love is this fastening into union. It cannot possibly exist amongst those outside of Christ, for they are connected by intellect, agreement, and preferences, while the children of God are connected by the sharing of the highest life, "*Spirit.*" Such a spiritual other-worldly oneness is the intent of the cross. He divided the wall and made us one.

HIS WISDOM IN FELLOWSHIP

The fullness of the expression of Christ will not come into the world any other way than that which Jesus said the world will know us by, *"love for one another."* It is to come through a community of born-again individuals who love God and each other. In Ephesians 3:10, Paul tells us that all things were created in order that the Church would have a platform through which to communicate God's wisdom to the principalities of the air. That wisdom is namely, love, but a love of what kind? It is a love that lays its life down. We are a spiritual family with the most wonderful Father.

The Church, as an authentic spiritual community, is a people of common union, sharing spiritual communion, keeping a common unity. *"The Word of God never tells us to create unity but to keep it. Christ made us one at the cross."*[91] The rejection of the cross will cause a rejection of each other. The rejection of each other is a rejection of the cross. *"The Church is to perfect our wisdom and knowledge on how to live with each other"* (Art Katz, *True Fellowship*).[92]

One minister so convincingly stated, *"You don't gossip about the brothers you pray for."* I desire to press such an issue further and say, when you really pray for your brothers and with your brothers, in the presence of God, you will melt into them. You will genuinely care for their purpose. The house that we, as a spiritual family, live in is none other than a house of prayer (Matthew 21:13). Having been united in prayer, we will genuinely seek each other's best interest. We will genuinely prefer each other above ourselves. We melt together in the presence of God together. *"God Himself is a sweet company"* (Bonhoeffer)[93] so He reproduces the same. Jesus taught us to *"love one another"* (John 13:34).

It is my experience that when two individuals that are flowing with God's love come together, they automatically love one another with no strings attached, because its basis is not founded upon what each one has done or can do for each other, but because of what Jesus did for us, mystically making us one, and by the example He gave us on the cross. Jealousy is foreign to such love. Competition is dissolved, and self-promotion is exchanged for the promotion of your brother. Without this kind of united spiritual love, the devil will find a way in and insert a bomb to scatter us, wounded and injured.

MY EXPERIENCE OF SUCH SPIRIT SELFLESSNESS

Years ago I was blessed to work for a worldwide organization that is currently changing the world. I got hired on as a warehouse worker without an ounce of responsibility but to keep this warehouse clean. I heard that one of my dear brothers to whom I was melted together in the fires of the revival in Pensacola was looking for work. I instantly was filled with a desire to help him in any way that I could. I wanted to help him, not out of pity or responsibility, but because I loved him. So, I soaked the situation in prayer and brought his name and résumé before a leader in the organization. He was hired on immediately.

"Jealousy is foreign to such love. Competition is dissolved, and self-promotion is exchanged for the promotion of your brother."

This brother is a gold mine of a person, and I knew that he would excel fast. It was not long after that I was moved again in my heart for him. Though he was doing well, in love for him, I was moved with a desire to see him excel further into what I knew he was called to do, and I approached the CEO of the organization with a strong swing for him. I knew no one more capable of running that whole organization and taking it further than it had yet been than my dear brother. I openly spoke for him, without him knowing. Needless to say, God ended up moving the CEO's heart to not only take him in, but eventually give him the whole company.

During this time I was let go, and went into the only field of work that I could find, which was construction. And anyone who knows anything about construction knows that it is not an ideal workplace, especially for a man who wants to live holy. A few years later, I visited my dear brother when I was driving by his office one day. I can still see the scene; he had an office looking exactly as you would imagine a CEO's office of a massive multi-country organization would look. He had a personal assistant and the world at his fingertips. There I sat in his beautiful office, while in my own life I was in a far less ideal situation, worn out and tired from constructions ways. And, being completely honest before the Lord, everything inside of me was so happy for him and proud of him that I could have cried in front of him. But I saved my tears for the car ride home. There wasn't an ounce of jealousy or competition or desire to be recompensed in any fashion. I was honestly and completely strengthened and encouraged by seeing him and his situation flourishing and moving forward.

This story is the product of divine love, the mixture of the union of the Spirit, and the effects of the cross.

I could never have mustered up enough love for someone to genuinely care for them without a touch of personal ambition. That is not natural. It is the Holy Spirit. Such a love and union by the Spirit that crushes competition, suspicion, personal ambition, doctrinal differences, and personality preferences must flow through the Church. As you see, this man is taking the organization to new heights, and that was God's plan. I am humbled to have even the smallest part in such a situation. Do you see that this is how God works? He relies on our surrender to Him to be able to maneuver things quickly. Some things take forever to come to pass because they are stopped up with envy and strife and selfish ambition. But, such a selfless love is the product of the cross. It feels strange using myself as an example of this, but I know that it had nothing to do with me. God wanted him there and God touched my wicked heart to love my brother with Godly love. All we have to do is stay fixed upon Jesus and such will be the case between each of us, if we can see that Jesus died for such a love and allow the Holy Spirit to simply perform it, by getting out of the way and laying down ourselves. Not only will it destroy the weeds that seek to choke out divine love and its product of unity, but it will also birth a supernatural longing to be together.

BEING TOGETHER

"The fruit of the Spirit is love" (Galatians 5). At the revival in Pensacola, I got right with God and was immediately

connected with others who were right with God and we gravitated toward each other, burning for Jesus and one another. This is the product of revival or the outpouring of the Holy Spirit.

"Pride is the heart of a distance and solitude that rejects the love of others." There was a brotherhood created among us that was deeper than blood. Jesus said, *"My... brother is He who does the will of God"* (Mark 3:35). Those born of God are now the children of God, born of His Spirit and washed in His blood. We have an eternal connection with each other. Because of this, we are IN one another. We actually NEED one another. We will always be together. I know that we will not experience such deepness, which I have described, with all members of the Body, for time would fail us before we could. But, we must grab those around us and hold them near and dear under the headship of Christ flowing down through the apostolic covering of more seasoned men ordained by God as leaders. It is important.

As the whole of the body will be affected and strengthen as each immediate joint connects together, we should never neglect getting together (Hebrews 10:25). Actually, something is wrong if we do neglect spiritual fellowship. Proverbs tells us that the man who *"isolates himself seeks his own desire and quarrels against all sound wisdom"* (Proverbs 18:1). Pride is the heart of a distance and solitude that rejects the love of others. *"Only by pride comes contention"* (Proverbs 13:10).

DIVERSITY

We should desire each other and also what each individual can bring to the whole puzzle. We should never get so "earthly" with each other that we encourage one another's flesh. But, in seeing one another after the Spirit, we are able to lift one another up to God and encourage each other's gifts (even if they are not like our own).

"No wonder divine melting love is foreign to the modern Church system. We are living like mere men instead of the spiritual conduits that we are to each other's lives."

The Church is not a building or place of worship. It is the new race (1 Corinthians 10:32). Those believers in your sphere of influence are the only other people around you who share your mind-set, purpose, and love for Him who died. It is my personal belief that we will be held accountable for what we did with and how we handled the brothers that God has placed around us, and those to whom we are divinely connected.

Prayer with each other is the heat of the presence of God that melts us together in purpose, focus, and burden. We must pray together. We must tackle issues of life together. We must break things open together in prayer. Fasting together is such a powerful thing; we need to live this way. We should be so connected together in prayer, fasting, fellowship, communion, and strengthening each other with spiritual gifts, that we are strong, united, and burdened enough to give our existence to preaching the Gospel in the world. There is no time for foolishness.

THE PROBLEM IN COMING TOGETHER

If we are not personally immersed in God we will be of little value to other people. If God does not consume us, when we are alone, we will not be consumed by Him together. If our personal time is spent in wasting time and the fluff of entertainment and worthless things, we will have a hard time living together in an eternal serious mind-set. The problem that I am seeing is that the Church is playing video games together instead of praying together. The Church is playing sports or watching sports together instead of preaching the Gospel together. The Church today would much rather call a poker night than a season of extended prayer and fasting for the city. No wonder there is strife and self-ambition, competition, and dissensions. No wonder divine melting love is foreign to the modern Church system. We are living like mere men instead of the spiritual conduits that we are to each other's lives.

Without genuine spiritual vitality amongst us we are not operating as a spiritual community. Without spiritual vitality we turn into a collection of friends staying out of trouble. Or a social club membership. There will be no spiritual union or divine melting through hours of movie nights or football. Community is spiritual union as we deliver Christ to each other and to the world together. A pizza night with two movies and a prayer is the evidence of an apathetic complacency that will eventually spiral into sin, division, selfishness, and death to the unity.

FULLNESS IN HIM

We tend to gravitate only toward those who are as fleshly as we are, as spiritual as we are, or gifted in the same way. May God destroy partiality and bring in a flood of divine love for one another, connecting us as brothers who do the will of God, reaching to this world in prayer, fasting, true spiritual fellowship, and preaching the Gospel.

"There is no other way, for the way, to be the way, than the way, the way was, when it was the way."

The first Church was not perfect, but they shared their lives together. We are not after perfection, because we are all flawed. The perfect bond isn't flawlessness, but the protection of love toward one another that covers a multitude of sins, rebukes each other's sins, and works through each other's sins. The first fruits of the Holy Spirit's outpouring show us the heart of God for His people. I am convinced that the Holy Spirit upon our lives will create the same today. The social club ways of many modern churches is an evidence of the need for a fresh baptism of the Holy Spirit.

We must allow the Spirit of God to move us in love for one another beyond our natural tendency. We need a closer life. Many men of God have fallen because there was no brother doing the will of God by his side and burning with enough love for him to look into his eyes on a regular basis and see if his heart was compromising.

Most church systems in America today are an environment where men can satisfy a religious itch, get an ounce of God, and hide from any real dealing with their personal issues. Not only will this never manifest the oneness that Jesus wanted amongst His own (John 17:22), but it will also cause an inoculation toward the real desire of God for His people.

PRACTICALLY SPEAKING

"We need a core group of people to look at face-to-face and share Jesus with and receive Jesus from." Practically, we should have at least one strong (preferably stronger than you) brother to talk to every day, if not see every day. We need a core group of people to look at face-to-face and share Jesus with and receive Jesus from. The fullest picture of Christ is released in the assembly when every member brings from his heart that which the Holy Spirit is impressing upon him.

Some would say, "I am just fine and I have never had such a thing in my life." Well, to such a thought I would reply, "What if you did? How much further along the path do you think you could have been had you listened to the passion of God's heart for His people? Even if you feel there would be no benefit, what about the fact that God expressed His desire for it to be a reality amongst His own?"

We love the open participatory place of house-to-house worship, but we must never substitute that for the devotion to the apostles' leadership and teaching in Solomon's temple.

System churches in America are important to have: the structure, the leadership, the service. It is all good and to a degree necessary. But, it cannot be a substitute for the authentic Christian love or community as I have defined it above.

We need both. Some churches have implemented "cell groups," which is a step in the right direction to take the community deeper into each other's lives; but without the power of the Holy Spirit resting upon it, they will end up acting like Adam (the old man) with each other under the banner of Christ's community.

The Scriptures tell us that there exists one Body but many members: the hand and the eye, the foot and the knee. We are fitly joined together and have a part of the whole. We must not look *"When a person who is evangelistic meets with him who is pastoral, they need the love of Jesus to see each other's sides."* down on the gifts or emphases of others. We must respect them and let them grow in their area. When a person who is evangelistic meets with him who is pastoral, they need the love of Jesus to see each other's sides.

It is like two blind men on either side of an elephant. One is holding the massive trunk of the elephant and describing it to the one holding the elephant's small tale. They must trust each other, and hear each other, to be able to put together what animal it is. If they insist on their feeling alone, they will divide. They must simply feel their side and listen to the other.

God gives us to each other and gives to us through each other. Robert Gladstone told me that when two men pray for bread, God might give one man two loaves and the other none. The man with two says, *"God, why didn't you give him one of these loaves?"* And God says, *"I did, when I gave it to you."* The cross is applied in fellowship. Robert Gladstone also told us about a time when God said to him concerning bearing the cross in relationships around him, *"I want you to die (to yourself) and don't worry...I am sending people to help you."*

Oh brothers and sisters, *"Unless we come into something that God can call community, we will not (express the) defeat (of) the powers of the air"*[94] (emphasis added). A oneness in Jesus, by the love of God, shedding a broad love in our hearts is the only thing that can display the wonderful fullness of Jesus in the earth and consequently demonstrate the wisdom above all wisdoms personified by Jesus on the cross that manifests the victories at Calvary.

Allow me to leave this chapter with a piece from Dietrich Bonhoeffer's work, *Christ In Community*:

"Christianity means community through Jesus Christ. We belong to each other only through and in Jesus Christ. What does this mean? It means, first, that the Christian needs others because of Jesus Christ. It means, second, that a Christian comes to others only through Jesus Christ. It means, third, that in Jesus Christ we have been chosen from eternity, accepted in time, and united for all eternity... without Christ there is discord between God and man and between man and man. Christ became the Mediator, and made peace with God and among men...without Christ we also could not know our brother, nor could we come to him. The way is blocked by our own ego. Christ opened the way to God and to our brother. Now Christians can live with one another in peace; they can become one...only by way of Jesus Christ are we one; only through Him are we bound together. To eternity, He remains the one Mediator. He who looks upon his brother should know that he will be eternally united with him in Jesus Christ. Christian community means community in and through Jesus Christ. The more genuine and the deeper our community becomes, the more will everything else between us recede; the more clearly and purely will Jesus Christ and His work become the one and only thing that is vital between us. We have one another only through Christ, but through Christ we do have one another, wholly, and for all eternity. Christian brotherhood is not an ideal, which we must realize; it is rather a reality created by God in Christ in which we may participate.

—⁓—

"By meditating upon Christ's humility, we shall see how far we are from being humble." ~Teresa of Avila

"A twisted crown of thorns, too small in size, was pressed into His brow and blood flowed in His eyes, blinding Him to all but the prize. He reduced himself to be despised; they split His back and exposed His insides. This is humility personified and the blood of God not realized. And though men love things that are deified, not a God who is crucified, but like a lamb to the slaughter without a sigh, that's my God. He comes; He dies." ~Eric William Gilmour

"The Eternal King was covered in the saliva of men. Have you ever been spat on?" ~Michael Koulianos

"Will you follow Me and take up your cross that others might see My image in you?" ~Mother Basilea Schlink

"When Christ bids a man, He bids him, 'Come and die.'" ~Dietrich Bonhoeffer

"Sanctification means an increasing participation in Christ's death." ~Benny Hinn

"The cross aligns me with what I am and protects me from what I was." ~Eric William Gilmour

—⁓—

CHAPTER 8

BURNING CROSS

"...To know Jesus Christ and Him crucified is not the minimum of knowledge but the maximum of knowledge; it is not to know little, but to know all; that here is not a descent from a loftier region, but an elevation into the highest sanctuary; that 'in Jesus Christ and Him crucified' all doctrines, all God's teachings, and man's experiences culminate; and from 'Jesus Christ and Him crucified' all duties, all works, all ministries are to emanate and to be evolved. Here is the hidden, the perfect wisdom of God. No doctrine is seen clearly and truly unless it leads to the cross; no work is God-pleasing, no experience or attainment genuine and vital, unless it has its source, root, and strength in the cross; no waiting for the second Advent is healthy and purifying unless it is called forth by the contemplation of the great God and Savior, who gave Himself for us, and redeemed us from all iniquity. He

who longs after wisdom, deep and broad, profound and comprehensive, lofty and real, heavenly and entering into the earthly life, let him learn from the Apostle Paul, that to know Jesus Christ and Him crucified is Alpha and Omega, that here are hid all treasures of wisdom, and knowledge, and spiritual understanding. No other fervor or activity is pleasing to God and useful on earth, but that which proceeds from beholding the Lamb that was slain. That which appears to the world as an obstacle is a channel, for the weakness of God is stronger than man. Idolatry substitutes ideas and things for the Divine Person. The world speaks of the true, the good, the beautiful; an element, an abstraction. This is not the language of revelation. The pagan asks, 'What?' The God-taught ask, 'Who?' Ideas however sublime, laws, however pure, cannot bring peace to the heart and life to the soul. Salvation can only come through a Savior; life can only be given from the source of life, the living God. And this is the greatest mystery of Godliness, that God Himself has come down to earth; that God Himself has visited His people; that the Son of God became man, 'God manifest in the flesh.' Higher than this we cannot rise. Greater gift than this God could not bestow on us. The Eternal has allied Himself with our finite existence."

~*Adolph Saphir,* Christ Crucified: Lectures on
First Corinthians Two (1873)

By what means did God choose to destroy the forces of evil that had ransacked a portion of His glory through their pride (Isaiah 14 and Ezekiel 28)? By what power will God reconcile all things to their rightful places? What does God see fit to right every wrong, destroy the power of evil influence, and align all things in their proper order, in response to such chaos wrought by pride, sin, and death? It is by no other means than the cross of Christ. It was always His plan because, *"the Lamb was slain before the foundations of the earth"* (Revelation 13:8; Acts 2:23). After the angelic rebellion against Him by pride, His divine plan to replace those rulers was to display to them the fact that His heart, rule, and character are nothing like them, by the glorious cross. In which, His plan was executed to both remove them from their places by showing forth His character and quickening those who would believe in Him by casting themselves upon His cross to rule in their stead. The principalities didn't know His wisdom of love in selfless humility, the demonstration of which was a power above all powers, stripping these powerful angelic rulers of all their power.

THE WISDOM OF GOD

In the first book of Corinthians in chapter 2, we see written, *"...We speak wisdom...a wisdom not of this world, nor of the rulers of this world, who are coming to naught: but we speak God's wisdom in a mystery, even the wisdom that hath been hidden, which God foreordained before the worlds unto our glory: which none of the rulers of this world hath known: for had they known it, they would not have **crucified** the Lord of glory."*

The wisdom is unmistakably united with the cross. This is the wisdom that Paul says is not *"of this world,"* and that the *"rulers of this world"* did not know. This wisdom is an octave too high for human and angelic ears. It is a wisdom that God is. It is a wisdom that cannot be transcended. It is the highest wisdom. It cannot be defined. It can only be demonstrated. The demonstration of such wisdom was so powerful that it was the only choice weapon of God to dethrone all evil powers and simultaneously reconcile the world to Himself. The cross, what precedes it, what it was, what it displays, what it accomplished, and what it will bring about, is the whole of understanding life. It is the secret to love, unity, power, wisdom, grace, mercy, favor, and eternity. The cross is the crux.

"The demonstration of such wisdom was so powerful that it was the only choice weapon of God to dethrone all evil powers and simultaneously reconcile the world to Himself."

My daughter and I built a small tent in the living room one night to sleep in. I used all kinds of things to prop it up and stabilize it. But the main installation upon which everything else was dependant was a big bar that was holding everything together. At one point my daughter wanted to remove it, because it was an eyesore to her as she was decorating the inside of the tent. As soon as she grabbed it and pulled it out, the whole tent came tumbling down. That glorious tent that resembled a castle was reduced to a bunch of pillows and sheets in a moment's time, all because she removed the heart upon which all things rested. The cross is the heart of the Christian life. *"If we remove the cross, we get lost."*[95] The cross is the unswerving standard to which everything must be aligned. It is the wisdom of God demonstrated. It is the power of God exercised. It is the revelation of what kind of heart the Father has. It is the centerpiece for time and eternity.

GOD BECAME A MAN

Let me press this a little deeper for us. It is so easy to think upon the cross or hear it mentioned in passing and simply give a silent nod to its action and accomplishment. It is easy to watch the *The Passion of the Christ* movie by Mel Gibson and think, *"Man, that is terrible."* But a careful meditation upon the cross will reveal that such a chosen humiliation entailed far more that what can be seen upon the surface of His sufferings. Come with me to a deeper meditation of His sufferings on our behalf.

He is the highest Supreme Being that there is, before whom there is none and there is none after Him. He holds all things together by the power of His Word and His sovereignty reigns over all things. He creates by speaking; He exists outside of time and He dwells in unapproachable light. None have seen Him nor can He be seen. He is far above all reason and dwells in an unknowable place. By Him all things are and without Him there is nothing. He alone is GOD. And this cross was God's choice to display His character for all to see. His wisdom of love in selflessness and humility is so powerful that its demonstration destroyed all evil and reconciled all of heaven and earth to Him. This is amazing! By just the simple display of His character He eradicated all evil, suffering, and death, and reconciled all things into their proper place. The cross is the divine response to the spinning chaos set in motion by the darkness of pride. God opens His heart to show forth the light of His Person and consequently righting all wrongs and dispelling all darkness.

The demonstration of Himself, through which He accomplished such a redeeming reconciliation and fashioning for Himself a replacement rule in the heavens, is that He laid aside His glorious God-ness and reduced Himself to become a man. GOD BECAME A MAN. Don't let such a statement pass over your mind without a pause to allow it to sink in. Read it again…the Creator of the ever-expanding universe and the One in Whom all things consist, the One and Only All Supreme Being that there is…WILLFULLY subjected Himself to the restrictions and frailty of a human body. If He stopped at that point, it would still be too much for us to grasp or comprehend. It would still be the greatest humiliation unparalleled to anything that man could even conjure up. Why? Well, let us delve deep into what it actually means for GOD TO BECOME A MAN. Don't miss the fact that in becoming a man you must first be a child. God, who put the whole world together, humbled Himself to be emptied of knowledge, so that humans must teach Him. God had to be taught how to read and write. God was taught how to sound out words. Does that not move you? Let us go further; before you are a child you are an infant. Have you ever had a child of your own? They are utterly dependant upon you for life. If you don't feed them, they die. They cannot walk, they cannot speak, and they cannot even exist without the continued aid of another. God reduced Himself. God...emptied, venerable, weak, frail, and dependent. GOD BECAME A MAN. Can we understand such things? But He didn't stop there.

A BLEEDING GOD

I am sure that the angels who couldn't come close to Him in glory without falling to their knees were baffled to tears at His chosen humiliation for man. Their pondering such things is recorded in Hebrews and Psalms, saying, *"What is*

"All the schooling in the world will never teach you that the greatest wisdom is not learned or recorded away in the mind, but demonstrated in selfless love. "

man...?" Can you see them looking at each other in shock and awe saying, *"What is He doing?"* There is not a fathomable scenario that comes close to comparison to what God chose to do on our behalf.

He gave Himself to an even greater humiliation. He allowed humans to bind His hands and feet. God, bound by man, unable to move. As I think of these things He did for me, His wisdom breaks my soul into a thousand pieces and melts them into vapors of worship.

God...tied to a rack and continuously tortured and ripped open. He, who never had been so low as to feel pain, came into our system of existence and reduced Himself to feel what we can feel. God felt His blood pour down His face, and I am sure His feet slipped on His own blood as He was forced to stand up after the body-splitting scourging. Do you know the feeling of seeing a large quantity of your own blood come out of your body onto the ground? It is our existence.

I want you to say this with me, "THE BLOOD OF GOD." The God-man was bleeding. God was mocked...openly for all to see. Don't forget that He was man. We reason it off as if He had no feelings and His memories of glory before the worlds were created were a consolation that removed Him from His present situation. Brothers, I tell you, He laid all of that down. He didn't stop there. He proceeded to the cross as a mocked, bloody, mangled human, for us. He gave Himself to the humiliating, naked, cursed death on a tree. Can you see the God-man there? Can you close your eyes and see God dripping blood by choice in a naked, humiliated, torturous death to save a people that hate Him? What kind of a God allows Himself to bleed to save rebellious, sinful mockers? This is unlike anything that there will ever be! This is love beyond comprehension. This is the highest wisdom that there is. This is the demonstration of His wisdom; the God of the universe loving us so much that He humbled Himself to death for a people who don't care about Him and are at war with Him.

God wins His battles by loving humility displayed to such a degree that it changes His enemies' hearts to fight for Him. *"God flexes His muscle by dying on a cross."*[96] Such wisdom the self centered, selfish, and prideful principalities couldn't understand. If they could have understood its heights of wisdom and power, they would never have aided His demonstration of the most powerful act ever to be performed; His love and selflessness is His demonstration of wisdom.

HUMILITY

All the schooling in the world will never teach you that the greatest wisdom is not learned or recorded away in the mind, but demonstrated in selfless love. He who loves most, is most wise. If there existed a book of wisdom, there would not be one recorded syllable from an old sage or a diagram drawn by the hand of Einstein or even a wondrous string of words from David or Paul, but simply a picture of the bloody God-man hanging on the cross. Oh, the humiliation of laying Himself down to be trampled, to save those who trample Him! You, who seek the depths of wisdom and to know all, look no further than this: God became a man to suffer and die to take our place and then resurrected to glory to raise us into the same. He sowed Himself down into the depths of the dirt, only to reach

"The self-life is that selfishness that steps in the way of the wisdom of God's selflessness being demonstrated through us."

the lowest of low, and in His ascent back into the heavens He gripped all mankind with His hand and pulled them up with Himself to glory. The glory of the cross cannot be seen in its totality until we who accept it into ourselves, as rule and life, are standing with Him in glory, ruling side by side upon His throne (Revelation 3:21; Daniel 7:26). Then, and only then, will the praise and glory of His grace, worked out by the cross, be understood (Ephesians 2:7). There exists a universal solution to all the problems of man, the Lamb that was slain. Whatever humiliation you are undergoing for the sake of Christ, remember, God became a man. If you are suffering in any fashion, been broken down by mockery or slander, remember, God became a man. There is nothing other than His wisdom that could have destroyed the powers of the air (Hebrews 2:14; Colossians 1:20,22; 2:15).

IDENTIFICATION WITH HIS CROSS

Now brothers, we are called to follow in His footsteps (1 Peter 2:21). In the letter to the Ephesians we see written, *"God who created all things; to the intent that now unto the principalities and the powers in the heavenly places might be made known through the church the manifold wisdom of God, according to the eternal purpose which He purposed in Christ Jesus our Lord"* (Ephesians 3:10-12).

God desires us to make known the same wisdom by demonstration of it in our lives as dethroning incense flowing up into the nostrils of the rulers of this world.

It was always His intent to display His wisdom and then quicken men to demonstrate the same by manifesting the character that was rejected by the prideful fallen rulers. Such will prove us worthy to ascend to replace them in the ages to come as we rule by His side forever and ever (Revelation 22:5).

Our identification with His cross is our choice. The fullness of the power of the cross to sever us from the dominion of sin and sickness and to deliver us from all the oppressions of the evil one are already purchased. His love has wonderful benefits. *"Forget not His benefits, who forgives all our iniquities and heals all of our diseases"* (Psalm 103:3). What wonderful effects of salvation: *"Surely our sicknesses He Himself bore...by His stripes we are healed"* (Isaiah 53:3-5). Everything that is not perfect health in your body was put upon Jesus at the cross. *"Sickness is to the body what sin is to the soul. It is already paid for by Christ Himself...every law that applies to salvation applies to healing"* (John G. Lake).[97] *"God cannot choose not to purchase your healing; He already bought it"* (Bill Johnson).[98] He is not questioning if He will buy your healing for you; He already bought it. It is God's will to heal everyone, of everything, at all times. God, in the Old Testament, was the healer (Exodus 15:26). In the New Testament, His

> *"The fullness of the power of the cross to sever us from the dominion of sin and sickness and to deliver us from all the oppressions of the evil one are already purchased."*

work as healer has been performed, making us the healed (1 Peter 2:24).[99] Some of the effects of the atonement are cleansing from sin, power over sin, healing from sickness, and power over sickness! The fullness of His love is not only shown to us in the suffering of His death for us as a substitute, but also in the realization of all the effects of that death. He entered into every part of man and reversed the poison of death that Adam's rebellion had set in motion.

TAKE UP YOUR CROSS

"Faith is this: the absolute refusing to trust in yourself and the casting of yourself totally upon Him. "

The end goal of everything is for us to be just like Jesus. He is *"bringing many sons unto glory..."* (Hebrews 2:10). The cross is the only instrument that He uses to fashion us into His image. Our cross is not a new one just for us, but the identification with His cross through surrender. Our cross is to identify with His cross. His cross deals with our sins; our cross is the continual identification with His cross that deals with the self-life. The self-life is that selfishness that steps in the way of the wisdom of God's selflessness being demonstrated through us. *God so loved the world that He gave His only Son so that whoever places his trust in Him would possess life* (John 3:16, my paraphrase). Faith is the essence of everything in God. Faith is this: the absolute refusing to trust in yourself and the casting of yourself totally upon Him. It is the cross! Faith and the cross are inseparable. They are synonymous. Why? Because faith is the resignation of yourself and the resignation of yourself is death, and total surrender is the faith of death igniting divine life! God did not nail His own hands down, but simply surrendered them to the nails. Our cross that taps us into the power of His cross, demonstrating the demon-dethroning power of God, is selfless surrender to the nails. Beware of any movement that excludes death to self. Death to self is the key to all the doors that we will enter and exit our entire Christian lives. The daily death to self is the only way to follow (Luke 9:23; Matthew 16:24). Nothing else will bring the resurrection power of the new life existence in God, causing us to demonstrate such wisdom in the world in keeping with God's eternal desire to show it through the Church to the fallen rulers, who are, even now, losing power and are about to be changed like an old garment (Hebrews 1:12).

CONCLUSION

The sad fact is, for the most part, the Church in the West has looked to everything else but the foolishness of the cross, preached in the power of the Spirit. I was in a local church, and an amazing thing struck me as I sat back and watched the presentation of the Sunday morning service. In the midst of multicolored blinking lights, coupled with smoke, a massive flat screen flashing modern art while the "worship leader" leaped onto the front pews singing into the camera, my little daughter said something to me in her innocence that struck my heart. Though I am not against using our artistic gifts to lift up the name of Jesus, this particular situation was a prophetic picture that was etched into my heart. My four-year-old daughter was mesmerized at the fast-paced busyness of the whole presentation. In the midst of it, she tapped me on my shoulder and asked a question I will never forget: "Daddy, where is Jesus?" Then, looking intently at the whole stage setup, she said to me, "There He is." I asked, "Where?" And she pointed my attention behind all the flash and glamour, to the dark, empty baptismal tank above which hung an old rugged cross. There were no lights shining from it. There was no smoke coming from it and it wasn't spinning. It was simply hanging there in the shadows, lost in the background of this expensive light-show concert in the name of Him who died. Behind the flash, left in the shadows, was the powerful wisdom of God, unattractive to man and overlooked by all, as the eyes of seraphs and cherubs, living creatures and archangels, flood the golden ground of heaven with confused tears, wondering why man doesn't understand how holy and sacred that old wooden cross truly is.

"It seems we have forgotten His wisdom, where the power lies, and where the glorious revelation of God is: in Jesus crucified and slain for all to see."

I am simply using this experience as a prophetic picture for the Western church. It seems we have forgotten His wisdom, where the power lies, and where the glorious revelation of God is: in Jesus crucified and slain for all to see. Let us make a resolution together, *"to know nothing among men, save Jesus Christ and Him crucified"* by surrendering our lives to death in response to His surrender unto death, that demonstrated His wisdom and reconciled all things to Himself by a single deathblow to darkness.

"A crown is of value for what it implies rather than what it is...He who despises a throne despises Him Who confers it." ~D.M. Panton

"Christ's cross is Christ's way to Christ's crown... No Cross, No Crown." ~William Penn

"The faculty of the soul that pants for Glory is implanted of God." ~Robert Govet

"...the sole legitimate ambition in the world — to be well-pleasing unto Him." ~Bengel

"What our eyes looked on, what our ears listened to, what our hearts loved, what our minds believed, what our lips said, what our hands wrought, where our feet walked — these are the unimpeachable evidences of the judgment seat. Secrets (1 Corinthians 4:5). Motives (Matthew 6:1). Soul attitudes (Luke 6:36-38)...the evidence wholly decides the award....Somewhere there exists a draft by the hand of God of what our lives might have been; let us find and live near to that divine original." ~D.M. Panton

"If you're not interested in ruling with Christ, you forfeit the very incentive to overcome." ~Art Katz

CHAPTER 9

BURNING HOPE

"The most glorious reward awaits such fidelity at the hour of Christ's return, while the heaviest punishment threatens the selfish indolence that would decline active employment of what it has received."
~Goebel

"Everyone who competes in the games goes into strict training. They do it to get a crown that will not last, but we do it to get a crown that will last forever."
~1 Corinthians 9:25

Our *"...affliction is producing for us...glory."* This future glory is *"far beyond all comparison"* to our present affliction, making it both *"momentary and light,"* regardless of the intensity (2 Corinthians 4:17; Romans 8:18; 2 Timothy 4:8; James 1:12). Those who have the *"eyes of their heart...enlightened,"* will *"know the hope* to which He has called us." This hope is spoken of as a *"glorious inheritance"* (Ephesians 1:18). The hope that we have is to one day receive the fullness of the inheritance. We are *"born again to a living hope…to obtain an inheritance which is imperishable and undefiled and will not fade away, reserved in heaven for us…"* (1 Peter 1:3-7). Notice that the inheritance is not heaven, but *"in heaven."* This is the *"…heavenly calling…"* (Hebrews 3:1).

SUFFERING

"…I consider that the sufferings of this present time are not worthy to be compared with the glory that is to be revealed to us."
~Romans 8:18

We have become partakers of the promises of Abraham by our faith placing us *"in Christ,"* who is Abraham's seed. Abraham's inheritance, though two-fold, heavenly and earthly, involves the earth (Romans 4:13); both spheres can be seen in Daniel 4:26; 10:13 (the heavens ruling over the earth). We are co-heirs with Christ, *"if indeed we share in His sufferings in order that we may also share in His glory"* (Romans 8:17). Christ's inheritance is *"the nations"* and *"ends of the earth His possession"* (Psalm 2:8). *"In this we greatly rejoice, even though now for a little while…you have been distressed by various trials…"* you *"may be found to result in…glory…at the revelation of Jesus Christ"* (1 Peter 1:6-8). It matters not what this life brings to us. As in Job's case, in uprightness (1:1), he despaired of life (17:1), suffered the loss of his servants (1:13), children

(1:18), health (2:7,13), wealth (1:16), and the loyalty of his wife (2:9). As he remained faithful through it all (13:15; 1:22), God brought Him into a restoration incomparable to what he previously had (42:10-15; James 5:11). *"...I consider that the sufferings of this present time are not worthy to be compared with the glory that is to be revealed to us"* (Romans 8:18).

"Dear friends, do not be surprised at the painful trial you are suffering, as though something strange were happening to you. But rejoice that you participate in the sufferings of Christ, so that you may be overjoyed when His glory is revealed" (1 Peter 4:12-13). That man who *"endures temptation/trials"* through obedience to Christ's commands (John 14:23), will be *"blessed"* by being *"approved,"* and when *"approved, he will receive the crown of life"* (James 1:12). Just because we, as Christians, are in line through Christ to obtain the fullness of the inheritance, doesn't mean that it cannot be forfeited. Esau

"The requirements of remaining faithful to receive a crown do not bend according to certain situations or individuals."

despised and gave up his inheritance for a temporal craving (Genesis 25:33-34). When he *"sought for the blessing with tears, he could bring about no change of mind"* and was *"rejected,"* with respect to the inheritance. Paul thought of the crown or approval of such value that he said, *"I discipline my body and make it my slave, so that...I myself will not be disapproved"* (1 Corinthians 9:24).

CHOOSING JESUS BY CHOOSING THE CROSS

It is our choice to *"come after"* Him. It is our decision to *"deny"* ourselves. Only we can choose to *"take up"* our *"cross."* But you *can be assured, if you "save"* your *"life,"* you *"will lose it." "For the Son of Man is going to come in His Father's glory with His angels, and then He will reward (just recompense; exact payment for services rendered) each person according to what he has done"* (whether good or bad (2 Corinthians 5:10; Matthew 16:24,27). Beloved, as far as fleshly lusts go, *"beat your body"* into submission by the power of the Spirit (1 Peter 1:22; Romans 8:11; 1 Corinthians 9:24). As far as suffering goes, *"endure"* (James 1:12). There is nothing else to say on the matter. Scripture simply leaves no room for explanation or excuse. There are no "special" cases. One either overcomes in his life or he does not. The requirements of remaining faithful to receive a crown do not bend according to certain situations or individuals. *"...It is required of stewards that one be found faithful"* (1 Corinthians 4:2).

STEWARDSHIP

Jesus spoke on this matter in the parables of the talents and pounds. Faithfulness was required of each servant at the return of the Master. Each servant was rewarded accordingly, both good and bad (Luke 19:11-26; Matthew 25:14-28). What is required of you is required of me, namely, faithfulness. Your life, whether you are sick, poor, rich, old, young, everything seems to go well, or you have countless areas that constantly collapse, it matters not. If you've lost everything, gained everything, been betrayed or befriended, it matters not. Affliction or peace, persecution or fame, money or poverty, IT MATTERS NOT! These things carry no weight, have no significance, hold no

"He who overcomes, I will give the right to sit with Me, even as I overcame and My Father gave Me the right to sit with Him."
~Revelation 3:21

relevance, for soon *"we must all appear before the judgment seat of Christ to give an account for the deeds that were done in the body, whether good, or bad"* (2 Corinthians 5:10). This judgment is for a specific purpose, namely, to prove who overcame. For, *"he who overcomes, I will give the right to sit with Me, even as I overcame and My Father gave Me the right to sit with Him"* (Revelation 3:21). *"He who overcomes I will give authority over the nations"* (Revelation 2:26). The overcoming Christians *"will receive a kingdom, and will possess it forever – yes, forever and ever"* (Daniel 7:18,22,27).

SUFFERING AND GLORY

The fulfillment of the creation of all things, the promises to Abraham, and the effects of the blood of the crucified Christ will be made manifest, reconciling all things to Himself (Colossians 1:16-19). All the *"kingdoms of this world"* will become the kingdoms of our God and His Christ (Revelation 11:15). Can you see it? This day when the promises to Abraham and the purpose for Adam become fulfilled through Christ ascending the throne with faithful men to rule the earth forever and ever? Is it real to you? Is it real enough to suffer for? Is it real enough to die for? Is it real enough to transform your mind to see any affliction in this life as something "momentary" and "light"? Is it such a reality and such a hope to you that any profit in this life is seen as "loss" or "rubbish"? Is it so real that you have no desire other than to "become like" Christ "in His death," to "share in His sufferings" so as to "attain" the resurrection out of the resurrected (Philippians 3:7-11)? Does the truth of the glory to come and sorrow of its loss cause you to weep for those who are not willing to receive it (Luke 13:34; 19:41-44; Mark 3:5)?

"Is it real enough to transform your mind to see any affliction in this life as something 'momentary' and 'light'?"

THE CALL

I issue a call to every Christian that exists! Every person who has passed from death unto life! Live worthy! He calls you into His glory and Kingdom! He calls you to rule by His side (Revelation 3:21; Ephesians 4:1; Colossians 1:10; 1 Thessalonians 2:12; Revelation 3:4). The magnitude and severity of this matter is beyond measure. I issue an incentive of future glory with Jesus and warning of its loss to every Christian! Awake! Stand up! Endure! Yield unto the power of the Spirit and gain the future glory of ruling with Jesus. If we choose not to yield, we will be fruitless before the Lord when He stands wanting fruit from our life (Ephesians 5:14-17; 1 John 2:28)! The incentive is the most glorious incentive that there will ever be — to rule by His side as a faithful Bride.

"To Him who overcomes I will give the right to sit with Me in My throne even as I overcame and My Father gave Me the right to sit with Him on His throne." ~Jesus Christ

"I am coming soon. My reward is with Me, and I will give to everyone according to what he has done." ~Jesus Christ

"Oh happy band of pilgrims, lift your eyes to the sky, where such a light affliction shall win so great a prize." ~G.H. Lang

"Christ will simply not say, 'Well done...' if it has not in fact been well done." ~G. Campbell Morgan

CHAPTER 10

BURNING BROTHERS

"REPENTANCE"

"What is repentance?"

*by.Brad**Shoeneck** & Eric**William**Gilmour*

(Evangelist/Revivalist)

Last week, I was sitting in a bright yellow waiting room, waiting for my Ford Taurus to get an oil change. While I was there, a minister who had fallen into sin a few years ago was on television. I couldn't help but watch, interested to hear his heart.

This was the second time I had seen him on TV since his moral failure, and every time I have seen him, he states that he has gone through extensive therapy and heavy counseling, and has finished the restoration process.

He is still married to his wife and finds himself struggling with thoughts of homosexuality to this day.

Concerning his failure, he states the classic line, "*No one is perfect and everyone makes mistakes.*"

No! Homosexuality is not a mistake. A mistake is when you forget to close the refrigerator door or forget to take out the trash. This was a gradual hardening of the heart that led to such a moral decline. A heart that has no conviction for lusting for a passing stranger is in a bad state; but a heart that enters a continual affair with a man is a heart that is need of a deeper work of the Spirit, especially because he was a minister of the Gospel (James 3:1). The red flag for me was that I never heard him mention the word *repentance* or *the power of God in his life to overcome,* or **most importantly**, *the blood of Jesus.* Nor did he mention taking every thought captive to the obedience of Christ or anything about putting off the old man and putting on the new (2 Corinthians 10:5; Romans 13:14). Is this horrible mind-set alive in other Christians living in America? Is there forgiveness without repentance? Read these words from William Booth's prophecy one hundred years ago.

> "*The chief danger of the 20th century will be religion without the Holy Ghost, Christianity without Christ, forgiveness without repentance, 'salvation' without regeneration, politics without God, and heaven without hell.*"

Notice in the middle, General Booth speaks of, *"forgiveness without repentance."* I believe in forgiveness and reconciliation to all, no matter what social class or level of wickedness they come from. But, there is a difference between what we have seen in this pastor and the repentance seen in the parable of the prodigal son (Luke chapter 15).

For those of us who are not familiar with the parable, there are **two sons**. The younger of the two said to his father, "Father, give me my portion of goods; my inheritance. I am entitled to the money that is to come to me" (paraphrased).

The Word of God states that not many days after that, the younger son gathered all his things together, took his journey into a far country, and wasted his substance with riotous living. And when he had spent all of his substance, there arose a mighty famine in the land and he began to be in want. His situation got so bad that he went and *joined himself* to a citizen or joined himself to a total stranger of that country; and he was sent into the citizen's fields to feed pigs.

Here is a young man who was once rich and now is in poverty. On top of that, there rose a mighty famine. Things have gotten so bad that he had to join himself to a citizen of that land. Here, the word "join" means, "to cleave to or to be glued together." It has the same meaning as when a man joins himself to a woman in marriage.

At this point the young man hits rock bottom, longing to fill his stomach with the food that the pigs were eating. In the preceding verse, it states that the young man *starts to come to his senses* and *he begins to remember* his father and his father's house. He asks himself, "Why am I here starving to death?"

I believe a lot of individuals, especially the young, are starving to death, maybe not from a physical hunger, but for **the Word of the Lord**. They are wondering, "Are there any absolutes in life?" There is an absolute in life. It is the Word of God.

In the book of Amos, it describes that there will come a day when there will be a famine, not of food or of thirst for water, but a famine of hearing the **Word of the Lord**. America is at this point.

"There are too many puppets and not enough prophets in the pulpits of America" (Leonard Ravenhill).

This young man heard the words of his father and he didn't cry out, "Father, I have made a mistake," or "Nobody is perfect." He cried out, *"I have sinned"* and *"I have sinned against God."* Not the Church. Not his family. But, "I have sinned against heaven and against God."

Notice the same response from David in Psalm 51, *"Against You and You only have I sinned."*

At this very point the restoration process began and the young man was restored to his father's house, and he was clothed in his right mind.

Now, back to the anonymous preacher. Not once during the interview did this pastor state that he sinned against God or against heaven. *He did not, at all, seem to be concerned about his relationship with Jesus.* How do I know that? Well, he didn't mention Him once. He spoke like a man who was only sorry because he got caught. I know this because his sorrow didn't cast him upon the blood of Jesus, but on a "restoration" process. *My friend, this is worldly sorrow, which leads to death.*

To the individual who is reading this, ask yourself, with a sincere heart, "Have I truly repented of my sins and turned to God? Do I really know Jesus? Do I really have a relationship with Jesus, not just with a church or a religion?" Jesus states that He is the **way**, and the **truth**, and the **life**. No one comes to the Father except through Him (John 14:6). Jesus is the door. Now I charge you to walk through Him, but before you do, **make sure you COMPLETELY close the door to your past**.

"Repentance must be a change of mind that produces a change of conduct and ends in salvation. Have you forsaken your sins? Or are you still practicing them? If so, you are still a sinner. You may have changed your mind, but if you have not changed your conduct, it is not Godly repentance.... False repentance is the sorrow of the world; sorrow for sin arising from worldly considerations and motives connected with the present life" (Charles Finney, *You Can Be Holy*).

"Jesus doesn't save you in your sins, but from your sins" (Dr. Michael L. Brown, *How Saved Are We?*).

"You say, 'When so and so preached, I got saved.' Well, what are you saved from? Are you saved from lying? Are you saved from cheating? Are you saved from lust? Are you saved from rebellion against your parents? Come on! What are you saved from?" (Leonard Ravenhill, Audio Messages)

"THE FRUIT OF FAITH"

"These people honor Me with their lips, but their hearts are far from Me. They worship Me in vain; their teachings are but rules taught by men." ~Matthew 15:7-9

*by.Scott**Howe***

(Founder of Evoke Concepts www.evokeministries.com)

We call this, "going through the motions." Most believers are simply going through the motions; offering up **lip service with no heart service**. Romans 10:9 says, "*Confess with your mouth AND believe in your heart.*" If you really do BELIEVE, then it will produce action. James wrote, "*Show me your faith by what you do*" (James 2:18), "*Don't just merely hear the Word, but do it*" (James 1:22)! Faith without action is **incomplete faith**, dead and useless (James 2:17). Even the demons believe (James 2:19). You could say that believing but not obeying is "demon-like faith."

John also warns us about this. "*If we CLAIM we have fellowship with God yet live in darkness, we are liars* (1 John 1)! *"If anyone CLAIMS to be in the light but hates his brother, he is really in darkness* (1 John 2:9). John makes it clear; there are those who claim to know God, and there are those who *possess fruit* of the fact that they know God.

Genuine faith produces action!

Your daily activities unveil the condition of your heart. Take an inventory of this week.

Do you spend hours watching TV but minutes in prayer?

Are you amused and preoccupied with movies and video games, but hardly interested in spiritual activities?

Do you study and recite sports stats with ease but can hardly recite portions of the Scripture?

Sadly, this is true for most of those who call themselves Christians in the Western world.

If we are not consumed with our God, living as exiles here on the earth, looking to our heavenly homeland, desiring for His kingdom to come...our faith is dead.

"Not everyone who SAYS to me, 'Lord, Lord,' will enter the Kingdom of heaven, but only those who do the will of My Father" (Matthew 7:21). *"A healthy tree bears good fruit. Every tree that does not bear good fruit is cut down and thrown in the fire"* (Matthew 7:18,19).

We have lowered the bar to an embarrassingly low height and call it the Christian life.

These are some of God's standards:

*"If anyone would come after Me, **he must deny himself and take up his cross and follow Me.** For whoever wants to save his life will lose it, but whoever loses his life for Me and for the Gospel will save it"* (Mark 8:34,35).

"Prepare your minds for action; be self-controlled. Do not conform to the evil desires you had when you lived in ignorance. Be holy in all you do" (1 Peter 1:13-15).

*"Therefore, since Christ suffered in His body, arm yourselves also with the same attitude, because he who has suffered in his body is done with sin. As a result, he does not live the rest of his earthly life for evil human desires, but rather for **the will of God."** (1 Peter 3:1,2).

"Go into all the world and preach *the good news to all creation. In My name they will drive out demons; they will speak in new tongues; they will place their hands on sick people, and they will get well"* (Mark 16:15).

It is very possible to sit in church and claim to have faith and even participate in activities once in a while, yet have a "dead faith," which does not produce any evidence that you have passed from death unto life...at all!

Faith in our hearts is evident by the fruit in our lives, not just by what we intellectually acknowledge to be true.

God knew this would be the standard of our day and in these few examples has warned us through Jesus, James, John, and Matthew. DO NOT BE DECEIVED! **You can only really know what you believe by what** your actions reveal. **Your actions will reveal to you with clarity and precision your spiritual condition.** Your heart is deceitful (Jeremiah 17:9) but **your actions speak loud and clear.**

I urge you! Take an inventory of your time spent and review your own actions. Confess your worldly affections to the Lord; the things that capture your heart and time that have no eternal significance. Repent of your sins. Cry out in prayer for sobriety and clarity of mind! Ask Him to consume your life with His life inside of you. No longer settle for the sham of a life that "religious" men produce. *Live for Him!* Be about His business! There is no need to have anything less than all power and authority by way of the Holy Spirit within you. God has made provision and you must make room for it.

We cannot walk as or with "said-faith" Christians any longer. Let your confession AND your FAITH be made complete by your actions (Luke 6:46-47)!

"SAVED TO SERVE"

"If I were to save your life, what would you do?"

*by.EvangelistDaniel**Kolenda***

(www.cfan.org)

This was the question that Cyrus, the King of Persia, asked to a rebel chieftain named Cagular whom he had captured and was about to execute. Cagular replied, "King, I would serve you the rest of my days." We would tend to see Cagular's pledge of allegiance and service to Cyrus as nothing more than a reasonable and expected obligation in exchange for the king's merciful pardon. *Cagular also recognized that because he was saved, he was compelled to serve.*

In Matthew chapter 8, we read that Peter's mother-in-law was ill with a fever. Jesus came to Peter's house, and verse 15 says, *"…He touched her hand, and the fever left her: and she arose, and ministered unto them."*

Mothers, grandmothers, and mothers-in-law…I guess they're all the same. If they're breathing, they're working. The moment that Peter's mother-in-law was able to get up, she was back in the kitchen, serving the guests and "ministering unto them." I probably would have said, "Relax, Mama! You've just been bedridden...you don't need to be waiting on house-guests right now! Let somebody else serve the tea and biscuits." But how could she just lie there? Jesus had touched her and healed her. *She felt obligated to get up and serve Him.* Notice that Jesus didn't stop her. In fact, perhaps He expected this reaction from the onset.

Paul told the Romans that they should present themselves to God as a living sacrifice, and then he added, "*This is your reasonable service.*" In other words, this is not some generous favor that you are doing for God. He purchased you and redeemed you with the blood of His Son. He set you free from sin and bondage. He has blessed you with every spiritual blessing in heavenly places in Christ. In light of all He has done for you, your reciprocal service to Him is only "reasonable." *You have been saved to serve.*

Mordecai told Esther, "Who knows but that you have come to the kingdom for such a time as this and for this very occasion?" In other words, Mordecai explained that Esther had been put in her position of power, prestige, and safety in the king's palace, *not because she was so beautiful or wonderful, but because God had a purpose for her to fulfill.*

Mordecai added, "If you keep silent at this time, relief and deliverance shall arise for the Jews from elsewhere, but you and your father's house will perish."

Her willingness to do her part in the fulfillment of that divine purpose was not a discretionary benevolence towards God – it was her obligation. She had been saved to serve.

Paul said in Romans 1:14 and 15, "I am a debtor both to the Greeks, and to the Barbarians; both to the wise, and to the unwise. So, as much as in me is, I am ready to preach the Gospel to you that are at Rome also." You see, the traditional thinking among the Jewish elite was that, as God's chosen people, any ministry to the gentiles was a magnanimous handout to undeserving heathen. But Paul saw himself as one who was shown great mercy by God and as such, a debtor to the rest of mankind. *For him to preach the Gospel to the gentiles was not a charitable condescension; it was his reasonable service, because Paul realized that he had been saved to serve.*

When Christ came, He came – for you. His perfect life He lived – for you. His tears, His sweat, His blood were – for you. The nails, the thorns, the whip, the cross, the grave, it was all – for you. If I were sitting on death row, condemned to die, and a merciful pardon arrived from the governor just before the moment of my execution, I would feel an overwhelming sense that I owed him my very life.

How much more, if he came himself and sat in my electric chair or stood before my firing squad or put his neck in my noose. If I were drowning, and you leaped into the seething ocean to save me, there would never be a day that passed when I would not remember you with deepest gratitude, and I would never allow even the slightest opportunity to serve you escape.

How ought we to respond to Christ who plunged into the deepest part of hell and wrenched us out of the very jaws of the devourer at the expense of His own precious life?

Our hearts should be set ablaze by this boundless mercy and selfless generosity.

Our lives should long to lie upon His altar. An American soldier in the Vietnam War was about to step on an antipersonnel land mine that was hidden from his sight. His comrade across the battlefield who could see the impending disaster from his vantage point stood up from behind his protective barricade and shouted a lifesaving warning to his friend. At that moment the brave young man received a fatal gunshot wound that would ultimately end his life. A couple of years later, at an honorary memorial service in the United States, the soldier whose life had been saved from the land mine had a chance to meet the family of his deceased friend. The son was only seven years old and had never gotten a chance to know his father.

"I want you to know," the soldier said to the young boy, *"Your father saved my life."*

The little boy looked up at him with tears streaming down his cheeks. "Sir," he said, *"were you worth it?"*

Leonard Ravenhill once asked the question, *"Is what you're living for worth Christ dying for?"*

He didn't save us so that we could be polished, decorative knickknacks sitting on His shelf, filling space in heaven for eternity. We have been saved for a purpose, and the fulfillment of that purpose is the only acceptable reaction that we can have to "so great a salvation."

You have an obligation, a debt of gratitude, a compulsion, and a liability to the One who laid down His life for you. You have been saved not for salvation's sake, but you have been saved to serve. This is your reasonable service.

Note from the Author:

Daniel Kolenda is not even thirty years of age and has won over TEN MILLION people to Jesus. When he preaches there is such a demonstration of the Spirit and power through the Gospel that countless blind eyes and deaf ears are COMPLETELY RESTORED. The cripples walk, and AIDS, tumors, and cancers are DESTROYED. This year alone he has seen two dead kids raised to life. When he writes this article, it has come from one whose life is upon the altar and has received the divine response of FIRE.

"THE GOD-LIFE"

"Christ in you the hope of glory."
~Colossians 2:27

*By.David**Popovici***

(Teacher at FIRE Chicago)

We are deeply entrenched in sin, within the chaos of this present evil age, to the extent that our minds and hearts are dominated by the pleasures of life and desires for other things. All the while, the devil sees no distinction between the *sinful-wasteful* son, who despises his inheritance (while on his knees in the midst of the pig trough) and the religious-biblical scholar whose head is vastly larger than his heart.

What has been the desire of God from ages past?

What is the triumph of this Gospel that has kept joyous smiles on the faces of men while facing their death?

I believe the answer to both of these questions is the same; namely, **Christ in you, the hope of glory**.

Both sin and religion keep us from knowing God. From garments made of fig leaves to towers built to the heavens, mankind's attempts to reach and please God have fallen miserably short.

The reason we are in famine on this side of the cross and the New Covenant is simply because *we have not looked upon Him* deeply enough. *God's plan for man far exceeds the bettering of our lives now. God is not interested in making you a better person, seeing that you are predisposed to self-centered, humanistic living; but rather, He is pleased in filling you with Himself.*

Whether the arrogant and pompous or the depressed and suicidal, the issue is this: *man can't get past himself. He is born with his back to God, and is merely breathing to death.*

Jesus said to Peter, *"flesh and blood did not reveal this to you, but My Father who is in Heaven"* (Matthew 16).

It was only after Peter had eyes to see Jesus, that he could see himself as God had called him to be, *"I will give you the keys of the Kingdom...."*

In order to truly understand anything, we have to have a revelation of God. *God has fully revealed Himself for all to see in the Man Christ — Jesus. He is the exact representation and express image of God and His nature.*

"Jesus Christ is perfect theology" (Bill Johnson, Bethel Church in Redding, CA).

All arguments and debates on God are met at the roadblock of the Gospels. Throughout time God had revealed Himself by His mighty acts, through His holy prophets, and even the revelation of His names; yet never before has He fully revealed Himself as He has today in His Son, Jesus. All other faiths deviate from Full Gospel preaching at the same point, *"Who do you say that I am?"*

I am convinced that God dwelling in man was and is the greatest miracle of all time. The Word of God calls Jesus the last *Adam* – the man who came to reverse the curse placed on us because of the first Adam, by becoming a curse for us to bring us back to God.

He is not just the Savior from sins; He has forever become the perfect mediator and prototype man.

Jesus Christ is the prototype man!

The Incarnation was never meant to be a one-time event, but to be perpetuated in the lives of all who would repent and receive His Holy Spirit by faith.

We need a radical change of our definition and perception of God and ourselves! Jesus said, *"Unless a man is born again, he cannot see the Kingdom of heaven."* Paul, when praying for the Ephesian believers, prays that God would give to them the Spirit of wisdom and revelation and *open the eyes of their heart*, in order to know Him better and consequently, to know what they have been called to be (Ephesians 1:18); a revelation of God and in turn a revelation of what God has made us. "Jesus doesn't call us for what we are, but because of what He makes from us" (Reinhard Bonnke).

*God will not just hold us accountable for what we were, but for what we could have been in light of the **cross** and **Pentecost***.

"...There exists a draft by the hand of God of what our lives could have been...find and live near to that divine original" (D.M. Panton).

It is these two events that divide the New Testament from the Old.

The cross *forever separates you from your own will and this world.* Paul said, *"I am crucified to the world and the world to me...."*

Pentecost *imparts Him into you like nothing else can.* Madame Guyon said, *"The more we possess Him, the more we possess His traits."*

Jesus said when speaking on the parable of the sower, *"Do you not understand this parable? How will you understand any of the parables?"*

The parable of the sower, sowing the Word of God, is the most radically fundamental parable of all parables. Its end goal is seen in the parable of the mustard seed, which is small until it uproots all other plants/trees that challenge its pre-eminence.

What does that mean?

The Word of God when applied by radical obedience and single-mindedness will put to death in our hearts all that challenges His Lordship. All this is in view of God's predetermined plan to produce in us the image of His Son (Romans 8:29). Paul travailed in prayer for it.

"My children with whom I am again in labor until Christ is formed in you" (Galatians 4:19).

Martha was distracted and bothered by so many things, and all the while, the Creator was in the room. But Mary sat listening to the Resurrection and the Life. *We stop the process of growth when we disconnect from the vine,* and we disconnect from the vine when we no longer come to Him and allow His Words to abide within us and ultimately rule us.

We become what we behold. It is as we behold (as in a mirror) the glory of the Lord that we are transformed into that same image, and from glory to glory (1 Corinthians 3:18)!

God did not sow His Son to reap servants. He sowed His Son to reap sons.

Christ is the firstborn among many brethren (Romans 8:29). God is bringing many sons to glory (Hebrews 2:10).

And the tragedy in the Church today is that *His Bride is either disqualifying herself by her wasteful and selfish living, or by the fact that she has educated herself into unbelief.* Both are blind, wretched, poor, and naked in the eyes of Him with whom we have to give an account.

We must return to the cross and Pentecost; everything else is humanism!

When a man is confronted by the cross, he is exposed and naked, because in front of Him lies the Perfect One. It is because of sin He remains unrecognizable, but when that man repents and receives the Savior, he receives the right to become a son of God (John 1:12). In turn, it is when this man looks deep upon the resurrected and victorious Lord that he meets Him, in His occupation, as the one who *"will baptize in the Holy Spirit and Fire."*

And then that same man now receives the ability to act like a son (by the Holy Spirit).

Adam came and produced a race of sinners; Jesus came and produces a race of sons (Romans 8:11).

The separation between the first Adam and the last Adam is the dripping cross and a flame of fire.

The question I ask you is this…where do you currently stand?

The answer to your question is exactly what your heart is staring at.

The Spirit of God in a human body is what makes you a Christian; and in your pilgrimage on earth you are to become like the Son, and to whatever degree that you become like Jesus, to that degree you are glorified and remain forever.

The eyes of the heart see best in prayer, fasting, and the meditation of His Word, and still these things cannot become a substitute for obedience.

Jesus calls all His disciples to be fishers of men. He never called unto Himself a monastic movement, but men who find their purpose in Luke 4:18-22.

Today we have perfect programs but pathetic people. God never asked for our towers of Babel; they impress only man. He said, "I am the light of the world," and then told His disciple that they were to be also.

"God did not call us to merely reflect the light, but to be light" (Bill Johnson, Bethel Church, Redding, CA).

*The world is not in need of better or more educated preachers who have relevant messages, but **men who have become the message**.*

God called Ezekiel to be a prophet, which by definition means, *"a borrowed mouth."* In Ezekiel 3:1-4, God feeds Ezekiel the scroll that was to define his life and calling, and after he eats it, it fills his inner man; and then, he is commissioned to "go, stand, and speak!"

Jesus, in the same way, tells the crowds that unless they eat His flesh and drink His blood they cannot be His disciples. A more offensive picture might not be possible to a religious Jew, especially since the Law clearly states that the life lies in the blood. But it is clear that offending people was the least concern of Jesus, since He knew what man's greatest need was: the Life of God. He said, "I came to give you Life, and Life in abundance," not mere human existence as they knew it, but the **God-Life** (Greek: *Zoe*).

The angel in Revelation gives John a scroll to eat, which in turn becomes his calling and message to the Church. Jeremiah could not hold in the Word, which burned in him like a fire. So we know that Jesus calls all of His disciples to follow Him, and it is He that makes them fishers of men. *He makes us,* fishers of men.

The command remains to GO, and to give Jesus to the world. But, a man can never "go" until he has first "come" unto Jesus in fullness.

The Great Commission remains the stewardship of the Church of God. Christ-likeness is utmost devotion to the Father and the laying of your life down for men.

The last thing this world needs is more professional preachers. The world needs living epistles written by the Spirit of God and read and known by all men. This is the divine outcry of our generation.

Christian extremism that is marked by radical and holy obedience to God, supernatural love, and demonstrations of power, signs, and wonders, is the only product that God will stamp as "SPIRIT FILLED."

Anything else is a joke and only provokes the world to more mockery. Let everything else burn—I want to know JESUS and become like JESUS!

It is easy to ask the question...

"Where is the God of Elijah?"

It is harder to answer...

"Where are the Elijahs of God?"

Where are they? I am not talking about echoes that merely parrot doctrinal truths, but men who have been absorbed into Him and now are His message in the earth.

What separates us from every other faith in the world?

It is the living, tangible presence of God. If we lose that, we lose everything!

Men with no fish are not fishermen; you can call them something else, but don't call them fishermen. Whatever office you might be called to or gifted in, it is to set the captives free. Freely you have received; freely give.

"Beloved, for the sake of a lost and dying world, pay any price, get God's power, and set the prisoners free."
~John G. Lake

Man must swallow the message. It is not until it goes through your insides that it can take effect on you. *Only then will you start to look and sound like that which you ate. Ministry is no longer a burden, but the outflow of the inflow of God into your life.*

God's will remains the same; His union with you is His goal. When He comes and increases in you, then you decrease and die. And it is only then that He can be lifted up in you so that He might draw all men unto Himself.

"One of these days we will get sick and tired of the spiritual bankruptcy that we live in and the joke that our lives often are and we will get serious with God." ~John G. Lake

APPENDIX

MANIFESTATIONS OF GLORY

Encouraged by recent conversations, responses, and corrections from honest, honorable, and genuine lovers of Jesus, I seek to open my heart and vulnerably submit some thoughts on the subject of "gold dust," "oil," "feathers," and "heavenly manna." Though there are many other interesting manifestations of His glory, I choose these subjects of topic alone, simply because these are the only ones that I have personally experienced.

My heart hurts thinking that no matter how gentle or honest or loving and open I can be, I know some will still be offended and angry with me, even though I have absolutely no control or power of any kind to cause the appearing of such things out of nothing.

I offer this to the skeptical brother in Christ that I love so much. Regardless of where we stand on these issues, we are brothers—and should be ready to lay our lives down for each other (1 John 3:16).

I do not, in any way, want to insinuate that without such manifestations that one is of lesser spirituality or that one is of a lower quality of relationship with Christ. Many brothers far greater than I have never experienced such things. Many fathers in the faith, prophetic people, and giants that have gone on before us have never experienced such things. Such a fact brings me to the conclusion that to not have such manifestations in your life wouldn't indicate some kind of hindrance in your spiritual progress in the Kingdom. These manifestations are not an end or a goal or even an individual pursuit. They are simply a method of communication and manifestation to reveal His glory. We cannot see God or the realm in which He dwells, but we believe in it. Gold dust, manna, oil, and these physical manifestations are simply a transferring of real substance from His realm into ours. These are wonder-filled things. He performs signs pointing to Himself and His realm that are invisible to us. It encourages our faith in the unseen realm where God Himself abides.

I have often said to brothers to make sure that they understand my heart in such things, *"The sign may disappear, but the speaking lives forever. The gold dust may vanish, but did you experience His nearness? The feathers are really mesmerizing, but are you under the shadow of His wings? The oil is my favorite, but did you experience the anointing of the Holy Spirit? The manna is captivating, but did you eat the Bread of Heaven?*" So I will take some statements that have been written to me and try to humbly reconcile them with the vastness of God in a way that is both unveiling of His glory and simultaneously honoring the honesty of the questions. I understand questions about signs and wonders. Not too long ago I asked almost all of the same questions myself. But I have seen too much and experienced too many manifestations in His presence to question anymore. I wouldn't trade it for the world. It is precious. Even though I have been literally insulted by many on account of these things—I would rather go through that for the rest of my life than to never experience the sweet manifestations of His presence in my life. For my life, I have resolved, glory or death. I must have His face. I must experience Him more and more or I don't want to live. For me these things have been signs to me that He is hearing my heart.

GOLD DUST

The first time I saw gold dust, I was at my mother-in-law's house in Atlanta. I had taken three days to fast and be alone with Jesus all day without any human contact till nighttime. On the second day, about twelve hours into it, I was lying on the bed and meditating on John 7, "*If anyone thirsts, let him come to Me and drink...,*" and at 4 o'clock I got up off the bed to get my blood moving and I saw gold dust splattered on the wall over the left side (my side) of the bed. I was staring at it for a long time, trying to figure out where it came from. Then it dawned on me that it was supernatural after it completely disappeared right there. Now, the experience was breathtaking; I needed to know why He did that. So after talking it through with a couple brothers and meditating on the possibility of its meaning, I knew. It meant that the message of my life was going to change to satisfaction with the glory of God, through intimacy and rest. This message of satisfaction with His glory alone must go to the four corners of the earth. The bed represented intimacy or rest, gold represented glory, the text I was reading was satisfaction with Christ (John 7), and 4 o'clock meant the four corners of the earth. From that day on, all my desires shifted into this, without any effort on my part. It is now the grace upon my life to speak of such a glorious facet of the Christian life; satisfaction with the glory of God through intimacy and rest in Jesus.

HEAVENLY MANNA

The first time that I saw manna, I was also at my mother-in-law's house months later, visiting for Thanksgiving. I was in the basement with my little infant, watching her play, while reading Gordon Fee's book, *God's Empowering Presence,* which is a study on the person of the Spirit (pneumatology) in all the letters of Paul. It is the extended version of his book, *Paul, the Spirit, and the People of God.* While I was reading, a small, flat piece of squishy bead-like cracker fell right into the gutter of the book. After looking around and knowing that there was no one else in the basement but my daughter, I searched to see where it could have possibly come from and examined it to figure out what it was. When I concluded that it was supernatural, I ate it. I ate it because I wanted God to see how bad I want to be one with Him. If He sends me something from His realm, I want to be one with it. I then began to prayerfully ponder its meaning. Then it became clear. I believe that it fell on that book because God wants us to have a heavy, theological anchor in the midst of our intoxicating experience of the Spirit. Part of that foundational anchor is that it happened in the basement, the understructure of the house. It happened while I was watching my infant, which to me is the bridge between the two. Childlikeness is the way into the Kingdom experience and the protection from overcomplexity in theology. We must have a childlike grasp on the whole of Scripture as our understructure, deeply anchoring us in the reality of God in the midst of experiencing the person of the Spirit. Now could that little unknown substance have been stuck on the ceiling all night long and just happened to fall on my book when I was there in the morning? Maybe, but probably not. So if one would want to take that route — I will just say it was special to me. Whatever it was, it was supernatural to me.

FEATHERS

The first time I saw a feather fall, I was in my office, and it fell directly on to the keypad of my Mac laptop.

I instantly knew that it was time to finish my book on *"becoming the Jesus people."* It was a small, white feather in a room that was completely empty, because we were moving and had cleared the room totally out. I had gone in there to get away and pray, using my laptop as an iPod. Could it have come from a pillow? Maybe, but how did it fall randomly in midair onto my laptop? It is just too perfect to have been a feather continuously floating around in the empty room that decided to come down right at that moment. Plus, pillow feathers were not a common site in my house.

OIL

The first time that I saw oil I was in my prayer closet, and after my wife had called my name, I opened the door and began to speak with her from the threshold of the door. When I touched the threshold with my hand, oil was oozing out of the top and sides from inside the prayer closet. I told my wife to come over and feel it. She was tripping out. She smelled it and it smelled just like frankincense oil. We were both in shock and knew beyond a doubt that it was supernatural. As I sought out the meaning, I remembered the threshold in Exodus 12. The blood was placed on it to save the life. So I knew that the threshold represented my life. According to the common typology, the oil represented the precious Holy Spirit and the fact that it was flowing only on the inside; I was able to see His message. The anointing of the Spirit flows from inside of the secret place. He was solidifying for me again this wonderful truth: "Stay with Me in the secret place and the oil will ooze out." Now, could it have been oil that someone anointed my doorpost with at some point when I wasn't there? Maybe, but probably not, since no one goes back there but me and my family, and my six-year-old is too short to do it; nor does she know where my oil is. Could I have anointed the door myself and had forgotten that I did? Maybe, but I don't think my memory is that bad. So to me, it was precious and a lovely speaking of God to my heart.

THEOLOGY

These things are not a necessity, but they are an incredible, sweet experience of His voice and manifestation of His glory available to all of us. I desire that everyone would step into such glory or manifestations of His presence, but I know that it will most likely be a controversy that will never truly end. So dear reader, have mercy on me. Try to hear my heart as your brother — a fellow man who has chosen to place all of his trust in Jesus, the Son of God. I did not seek these things. I sought Him. He brought them to me. I cannot perform them; they simply manifest. I am not trying to build a case against a nonmanifestation mind-set. I simply want all of the Holy Spirit that I can get in this short life. I simply despise the "either-or" mentality; I want it all. Everything that the Christ has in Himself to reveal Himself to me and His body, I am all in. I can promise that it will encourage you and draw you closer to His side as His glory begins to materialize in your life and

He punctures you with His current speaking. The Holy Spirit reveals Jesus and Jesus reconciles us to God, the One and only true glorious Lover and Judge.

So I am asking for the benefit of the doubt. I am asking for an open and honest ear. I love Jesus, the only God-man and glorious Son of God. I preach Jesus and obey His Word, looking forward to His coming. With that limited understanding of my heart, please read on with a tender, gracious, loving, and open ear.

> *"God's ontological consistency is distinct from the diversity of ways in which He reveals himself...."*
> ~Dr. Jeff Hubing (President of FIRE School of ministry in Chicago, IL, March 2012)

Ontology is the branch of metaphysics that studies the nature of existence or being as such. In the context of the quote, the consistency of God's nature is distinct (meaning, not identical) with the diversity (difference) of ways in which He reveals Himself or makes Himself known. Throughout the whole of Scripture, it is more of a rarity that God would do the same thing twice, than He would do something different. Is that not the case? Look at the variation of the plagues in Exodus sent upon Egypt and Pharaoh. Are they not strange and distinct themselves: frogs, flies, hail, death, etc.? Why did He not send those same plagues into the land of Canaan to bring the children of Israel into the land of promise? Think of Daniel's life next to Job's. Or Abraham and Paul. Or Samson and Jeremiah. Elijah and John the Baptist. David and Noah. These various workings and ways are all the same God. My point is that He shows us in His Scripture not just what He did, what He will do, and what He can do, but most of all, what He is like. He is a person, a living individual in three glorious parts that are incredibly different themselves yet inseparable. He is not very predictable. Even Jesus Himself, the exact representation of the Father, never performed a miracle the same way. "Everything that Jesus did, He did as a man, to show us what the human life infused with divine life should look like" (Bill Johnson). He equally did everything, as God, to show us what God is truly like.

In seeing that Christ never did the same thing the same way twice, is it not a testimony of the distinct ways in which He reveals Himself and will reveal Himself today (Hebrews 13:8). Jesus' life shows us that the same perfectly consistent God who revealed Himself in a variation of ways through the Old Testament judges, prophets, kings, fathers, and the children of Israel, is the same way in the New Testament. The major difference is that today, everything that is done is all inside the person of Jesus Christ, meaning in and through a living relationship with Jesus through the Holy Spirit.

We all know that God can actually be known and not just known about. God's unchangeableness does not lock Him into a prison of only doing what He has done. But rather, He has always been unchangeable. He did not become unchangeable after the writing of Malachi 3:6. He was unchangeable before Genesis 1:1. Every one of the various workings of God, throughout the whole of Scripture, are performed by this same unchangeable God.

His glory is revealed in many ways, always pointing to the one Way, Jesus, the very glory of God Himself.

> *"God is revealing His glory visibly to many people. There have been times I was speaking that people couldn't even see me. They could only see the light of the glory of God. Many times people have told me that as I was preaching they saw a cloud form like the figure of a man and stand beside me as I a was ministering. The cloud has also been seen above me, beside me, behind me, in front of me, and engulfing me. Sometimes the glory comes down as dewdrops. Sometimes it comes down as golden drops of rain. Sometimes it comes as a pillar of cloud. Sometimes it comes as a pillar of fire. Some people see little sparkles....Some people see it as gray or yellow smoke. People see the glory manifest in many different ways. It doesn't matter exactly how you see it....The vocabulary with which we describe the glory isn't important (either). Experiencing it is. Let the glory come into the midst of the people of God, the glory of HIS presence"* (Ruth Ward Heflin, *Glory*, page 143).

It is commonly said that signs and wonders are, *"signs that make you wonder."* The definition of the word "*wonder,*" according to Noah Webster, is "*an amazement and awe, filled with admiration and curiosity.*" Things that are wonders in the Scriptures are things that could never have happened naturally. It is the supernatural activity of God. Think about the sun stopping for Joshua, the fire falling from heaven for Elijah, the stone killing a giant through David, the water out of a rock with Moses, the bitter waters made sweet by a tree, Samson killing thousands by himself, the temple filling with a cloud of glory and no one able to stand up, the fire by night, the manna from heaven, the quail, the raising of the dead with the apostles, the handkerchiefs with Paul, the transportation of Philip, the snakebite on Paul, the angelic visitations, all of the Theophanys, and many, many more. If we are going to lock ourselves into only what Scripture says, how do you justify moving to Miami according to the "Word of the Lord" when that specific speaking is not directly in the Scriptures? There is no dental work done in the New Testament. Does that mean God won't heal teeth? There is no falling out under the power of the Holy Spirit in the New Testament. Does that mean that is not God?

After I was rebuked by several people for a short video I placed on YouTube of gold dust, Dr. Jeff Hubing said these kind words about me—I include this for one reason; I think hidden in here are the major protection points for dealing with signs and wonders.

*"He is definitely aware of the **all-surpassing beauty of Jesus**, and has lived his life focused on eternity and **proclaiming the Gospel** in*

the present time. He just happens to have experiences like this, which are just a glimpse of that beauty to come. I think to discount it just because this specific thing does not appear in Scripture is a bit difficult to defend. Would you have said the same thing to Jesus and the disciples when they found the coin in the fish's mouth? That certainly never occurred in the Jewish Scriptures. I mean, it's one thing to **build a doctrine around an experience** (as in, 'Everyone must seek gold dust, or you are not experiencing God'). I reject that kind of construct as well. But, it's another thing to deny that God can do something just because He hasn't done it before ('God will not reveal Himself through gold dust because He never has previously'). I would suggest that God's ontological consistency (Hebrews 13:8) is distinct from the diversity of ways in which He reveals Himself, which are as varied as His own creativity."

One of my friends, Brian Guerin, the founder of Bridal Glory International, has had many more things like this happen to him than I have, and I can attest, he is an intense lover of Jesus. I don't know if I have ever met someone so lovesick for Jesus. He came and ministered here at my home church and all he did was cry and talk about intimacy with Jesus. He seeks God with all his heart and is burning with the Gospel. His book, *Modern Day Mysticism,* will rock anyone's world. After speaking to him concerning some of the slander and persecutions on my life for these things, he wrote the following to me:

> *"These brothers of ours who must have a biblical basis for everything God says or does seem to fear deception more than they trust the Holy Spirit's ability to lead them into all truth. And always remember, 'That which you fear most, you submit to most' (submission follows fear). So actually fearing deception will eventually lead you right under the authority of deception. Signs and wonders 'follow them that believe.' So 'fearing deception,' their doubting of signs and wonders causes them to never see signs and wonders follow them. We must become like a child to access the Kingdom realm, where these things just happen. If we think that we can confine the God of the universe, galaxies, heaven, and earth to one book, we have got to be kidding ourselves. It is actually antibiblical that everything must be found in the Scriptures. The higher standard is that God will never CONTRADICT Scripture, but to think we can confine Him to one book is nonsensical."*

Unbiblical is contradiction, contrary, and opposes what God has said. Extrabiblical is something that is supported by the Scripture, a supplement, and points to what God has already said. David Popovici, a teacher at FIRE School of Ministry in Chicago and founder of Kingdom Gospel Mission, made some really solid points in the following correspondence.

"There's a big difference between something not being in Scripture word for word and something being scriptural, or contrary to the very intent, revelation, and spirit of the Scriptures. For example, I remember back in the day a lot of folks would say, 'Where does it say that we can't smoke weed in the Bible?' Well, truth is, it is not in there, word for word. But it does say that your body is to be the temple of the Holy Ghost and that drunkenness is sin. So between these two, one can see that the Scriptures stand opposed to being under any influence of a substance except the Holy Spirit. In like manner, I would say for gold dust or other manifestations, that it does not contradict the revelation of Scripture at all; rather, it reveals something of God and His coming Kingdom. I think the only way one can potentially get in trouble with it is by losing focus, as it is with anything else; becoming obsessed with it instead of the Lord and what He's saying through it. But people like that are usually not too hard to spot, because if they are so easily distracted by signs and wonders, they're probably already off in a few other major areas of their life in God. I would emphasize Jesus, and signs and

*wonders as what He sends to invite us into a
deeper understanding and worship of Him."*

It is *"God...who does great and unsearchable things,
wonders without number* (Job 5:9). This word "unsearchable" is great, because it is saying that you can't even
begin to search to understand them, nor could you
ever find them all out. It is OK if we don't understand
everything about God. As Bill Johnson said, *"If we
understand everything about God, than we have a God that
looks a lot like us."* Who wants that? How often has God
done wondrous things? Think of your own life, when
He warned you through a dream or burned a vision in
your heart that no one can take away from you, yet it is
not specifically in Scripture. Gold dust from the Holy
Spirit, to make manifest His presence, is just another
one. But He isn't just doing it to say, *"Look, Mom, no
hands."* God is speaking, God is moving, and God is
communicating continuously, all through a living relationship with Jesus Christ.

I have learned much about these things from several
brothers who are experiencing them more consistently
than I have been. They are constantly telling me that
God does nothing arbitrarily. Heaven is ordered and
strategic. It is important to check the time and analyze
everything about the current situation when one of
these manifestations occurs, because God is trying to
say something. The mysterious wonder of a sign is set
up to get us to search out His voice. *"It is the glory of
God to conceal a matter and the glory of a king to search it
out"* (Proverbs 25:2). Think about this; regular signs in

the road point toward something, and the wonder of heavenly signs point to the voice of God, namely, Jesus Christ, the speaking of God. It is our knowledge of the Scriptures that helps unfold the interpretation of what He is saying. It was Madame Guyon who said, *"Above all things, God longs to communicate Himself."* That is exactly what He is doing through these manifestations of His glory.

A friend of mine, Michael Koulianos, was speaking with a Lutheran pastor named Paul Tesky, who has a tremendous healing and miracles ministry and often sees many wonders at his church, and his thought was clever. He said, *"Anyone can say that God is with them, but if He really is with them, He will show it somehow."* I love what Roland Baker said when he was asked why he loves signs and wonders, *"We love wonders because we love God. When you love someone, you love what they do."* How awesome are His ways! I have been told to be humble enough to not say anything when they happen, but that is not the way we are expected and even commanded to be concerning God's glorious ways. That is simply not the way a humble (obedient) lover and proclaimer of Christ is to live; we don't hide lights, we shine them. *"...speak of His wonders"* (1 Chronicles 16:9; Psalm 105:2; 26:7). Paul and Barnabas spoke of the signs and wonders that God did through them for the revelation of Jesus Christ (Acts 15:12). They are simply manifestations of His presence in the message.

"It has seemed good to me to declare the signs and wonders which the Most High God has done for me. How great are

*His signs and how mighty are His wonders! His kingdom is
an everlasting kingdom and His dominion is from generation to generation"* (Daniel 4:2-3).

Signs and wonders are actually part of God's attesta-
tion to His message and sent ones. Signs and wonders
are connected with the Gospel; the greatest message
and revelation of Jesus Christ (Romans 15-19).

Even Jesus was attested to by signs, wonders, and miracles (Acts 2:22). God uses these things as an attesta-
tion to His servants (2 Corinthians 12:12). Immediately
the question comes up in the mind of the thoughtful,
what about lying signs and wonders? What about the
miracles and wonders in Matthew 7:22? What about
the people seeing wonders and not knowing Jesus at
all (Matthew 7:22)? These people in context of Matthew
chapter 7 are those who are not obeying the will of God
(verse 21) and have no intimacy with Jesus (verse 22).

Signs and wonders can be mimicked by the devil,
doubtless. But the dividing factor is exactly what is
shown to us; namely, a life that is not living according to
the will of God and having no real intimacy with Jesus.
In the New Testament lying signs and wonders are
connected with the spirit of antichrist (2 Thessalonians
2:9). There is simply no way to exalt the name of Jesus,
worship and adore Him as the one true God who came
as a man to die and take our place, and then resurrected
to sit at the right hand of the father, and wait to come
back to the earth and rule and reign, and be the spirit
of antichrist. Maybe the devil could deceive through

modern-day Gnosticism and its branches of Docetism and Cerinthianism, but definitely not through the Spirit that acknowledges that Jesus Christ has come in the flesh as God reconciling man to Himself (1 John 4:1-4).

In my personal experience, these wonders tend to happen out of extended times of intense adoration and worship. Kathy Walters was once asked, *"How do you get that gold dust to come upon you so often?"* She said, *"You have to learn how to relax, enjoy Jesus, and you must understand grace."*

There was an amazing outbreak of diamonds, gems, and oil in San Juan, Puerto Rico, at Pastor Denis Rojas' church. Concerning the appearance of the manifestations he said, *"It seems to depend upon the adoration of the people."* How precious is that! He loves to be adored by His own and He manifests Himself to them. When the diamonds were taken to a professional jeweler, the jeweler asked, *"Where did you get this?"* To which they replied, *"Why?"* And the jeweler said, *"Because there is none like it on the earth."*

Most people say, *"Don't be deceived."* I understand and am grateful for the warning, but 2 Thessalonians connects the lying wonders with lawlessness. Lawlessness plus wonders equals the devil. The Gospel of Jesus, from an intimate life with Christ, a holy life, and wonders, equals a manifestation of His glory. So for me it is pretty easy to tell lying wonders and glorious wonders.

Check list…

1. Are the wonders coming through or to a life that worships and adores Jesus Christ, the Son of God, who became man to suffer, resurrect, and will return to rule?

2. Are the wonders coming to or through a life that is in accordance with the will of God, obeying Jesus' words, and selflessly loving others?

3. Are the wonders coming to or through a life that is intimate with Jesus and promotes intimacy with Jesus?

All I am asking is this, does the person's message point you to adore, love, and serve Jesus? If the person is emphasizing wonders as some type of replacement for the Word of God or Christ—that is antichrist. That is a lying wonder. If a man is seeing wonders in his life but he simply will not submit to the truth of Jesus Christ's Gospel, those are lying wonders. If the man has no personal intimacy with Jesus and desire to adore and love Jesus, those are lying wonders. If the man is living like the devil and seeing wonders, I have a hard time believing that God endorses him. But yet, God may endorse some people that we don't. He is the only One with all the facts surrounding any given situation. God spoke to me one time and said, *"If you want to stop up the flow of My grace in your life, judge someone."* Now open sin is a different issue, but personality, personal preference, and shallow theological differences are petty.

209

It is my opinion that we should leave the box to the side and let God do whatever He wishes as we look to Jesus, do His will, and intimately seek Him. A friend of mine, Cody Duncan, an amazing prophetic worship leader, says, *"We need a box-burning session."* How true! What would God burn out of me? What would God burn out of you? How much of what we are holding on to is really a hindrance to more that God wants to use to reveal of Himself to us?

I have a couple last thoughts—many signs and wonders took place through the apostles (Acts 2:43). If we want to glue it to the apostles alone, than what do we do with Stephen, who was not an apostle, but a waiter of tables and was seeing many signs and wonders (Acts 6:8)? The early Church prayed for signs and wonders (Acts 4:30). Signs and wonders are a confirming of the message (Hebrews 2:4; Mark 16:17). Carlos Annacondia said, *"A church without signs and wonders is an incomplete church."* It doesn't matter what kind of signs and wonders; just actual manifestations of the person of the Spirit. They bring glory to the person of Jesus Christ. They are revealing His glory. They are sweet speakings from His realm. They are love tokens. My wife loves me more than the wedding ring I got her, but she still cherishes it, because it came from me and it symbolizes a vow between us.

To say that a man of deceit can distort them and turn them around for evil is not a very good argument, because a man can do that with any gift of the Spirit, or even the Scriptures themselves, and they have from the very beginning of the Church (Gal. 3:1). Let God be true and every man a liar. God will prevail, even in the midst of snakes mimicking His power; though at one point it looks like they are the same, He will end up swallowing them.

"For You are great and do wondrous deeds;
You alone are God."
~Psalm 86:10

"You are the God who works wonders;
You have made known Your strength among the peoples."
~Psalm 77:14

"Who is like You among the gods, O LORD?
Who is like You, majestic in holiness,
Awesome in praises, working wonders?"
~Exodus 15:11

ABOUT THE AUTHOR

 I met Jesus the first day that I saw Evangelist Steve Hill at Brownsville Assembly of God in Pensacola, Florida, in 1996. His face was radiating with light, and for the first time in my life, Jesus was manifested to me in the preaching of the cross in the power of the Spirit. I have not been the same since.

I graduated the Brownsville Revival School of Ministry in 2001, then returned to FIRE school of ministry to enter Dr. Michael L. Brown's mentoring group in 2002. In 2003 I started working at Christ for all Nations, the ministry of Reinhard Bonnke. I was married in 2004 to a beautiful woman who happened to be my closest friend in the world. Today we have two girls, Madison and Lia. I was laid off at CfaN in 2007 and started working construction till God spoke deep into my being in the summer of 2010. He said, "I want you to be my spokesman." After a two weeks' notice, I quit working construction and started giving my life to the Gospel alone. Since that day, God has been gracious to back His Gospel with signs, wonders, and miracles. Cancers, hepatitis, broken bones, and many more sicknesses have been crushed by the name of Jesus. Hundreds have surrendered their lives to Jesus in response to the Gospel. We are under a mandate from the Lord to set the captives free by the power of the Spirit. But the center of our hearts in God is to fuel the revolution of the Jesus people; seeking oneness with God through surrender, teaching on the inner life, the interior matters concerning the soul being dominated by the Spirit of God.

Those that are led by the Spirit are the sons of God. SONSHIP!

Eric William Gilmour
sonship-international.org
eric@sonship-international.org

ENDNOTES

1 C.H. Spurgeon, *Morning And Evening* (Christian Focus Publications).

2 I heard this in an audio message from Bill Johnson from Bethel Church's podcast, Redding, CA.

3 Christians who do not love Jesus only and except additions, in my opinion, have tolerated an obstruction to the wholehearted love for Jesus that the Holy Spirit placed inside of them when He sheds Himself abroad in their life. The issue is tolerated obstructions. It is not an issue of doing something more, but becoming less. Surrender is our seeking.

4 Audio message by Leonard Ravenhill. www.sermonindex.com

5 This is from Leonard Ravenhill, compilation called *Prayer.* www.agonypress.org

6 I was paraphrasing a quote from an Andrew Murray book called, *Absolute Surrender* (Whitaker House Publishers).

[7] Basilea Schlink, *My All for Him* (Bethany House Publishers).

[8] I use the word "Adamic" to depict the life is that life inherited by our fathers, passed down from Adam.

[9] *Webster's Dictionary.*

[10] Robert Gladstone has a great story behind this quote from an old, saintly Welshman named Earnest.

[11] S.J. Hill, *Enjoying God* (Relevant Books).

[12] Told by Dr. Michael L. Brown during school at Brownsville Revival School of Ministry.

[13] This is from an audio teaching from Kathryn Kuhlman. www.sermonindex.com

[14] Dr. Michael L. Brown, Holy Desperation message from Brownsville Assembly of God, 1999.

[15] Here are the lyrics from the complete hymn that was quoted.

Rock of Ages

Rock of Ages, cleft for me,
Let me hide myself in Thee;
Let the water and the blood,
From Thy wounded side which flowed,
Be of sin the double cure;
Save from wrath and make me pure.

Not the labor of my hands
Can fulfill Thy law's demands;
Could my zeal no respite know,
Could my tears forever flow,
All for sin could not atone;
Thou must save, and Thou alone.

Nothing in my hand I bring,
Simply to the cross I cling;
Naked, come to Thee for dress;
Helpless look to Thee for grace;
Foul, I to the fountain fly;
Wash me, Savior, or I die.

While I draw this fleeting breath,
When mine eyes shall close in death,
When I soar to worlds unknown,
See Thee on Thy judgment throne,
Rock of Ages, cleft for me,
Let me hide myself in Thee.

[16] Dietrich Bonhoeffer, Daily Devotional.

[17] St. Francis de Sales, *Introduction to the Devout Life* (Kessinger Publishing, LLC, May 31, 1942).

[18] David Ravenhill, taken from the audio of classes taught at FIRE Chicago.

[19] Robert Govet, *Reward According to Works* (Schoettle Publishing).

[20] Andrew Murray, *Humility* (Whitaker House Publishers).

[21] Paris Reidhead, "Ten Sheckles and a Shirt."

[22] Madame Guyon, *Experiencing the Depths of Jesus Christ* (Seed Sowers International).

[23] Leonard Ravenhill compilation called *Agony* from agonypress.org.

[24] *Webster's Dictionary.*

[25] A.W. Tozer, *The Pursuit of God* (Christian Publications, Inc.)

[26] *On Earth As It Is In Heaven,* compiled by Steve Hill (Together In The Harvest Ministries).

[27] Bill Johnson compilation, called *Heaven on Earth.* www.agonypress.org

[28] Benny Hinn, YouTube channel, "Bring Back the Cross."

[29] Meister Eckhart, *Encyclopedia of Christian Quotes.*

[30] I use the word "Adamic" to mean: from Adam; that which was inherited by your earthly father.

[31] Robert Gladstone said this in a Emerging Church class in 1999 and it never left me. I believe that class was changed to Apostolic Community so as not to be confused with the Emerging Church movement.

[32] Watchman Nee, *Spiritual Authority* (Christian Fellowship Publishers).

[33] David Popovici, Teacher at FIRE Chicago.

34 Oswald Chambers, *My Utmost For His Highest* (Discovery House Publishers).

35 That quote is partially from David Popovici, teacher at FIRE Chicago, and *When Heaven Invades Earth* by Bill Johnson.

36 Oswald Chambers, *My Utmost for His Highest* (Discovery House Publishers).

37 Bill Johnson quote from an audio message from the Bethel Church's podcast, Redding, CA.

38 I believe this was D.L. Moody.

39 I heard Keith Daniel say this in a sermon from a sermon index.

40 Leonard Ravenhill, *Why Revival Tarries* (Bethany House Publishers).

41 E.M. Bounds, *E.M. Bounds On Prayer* (Whitaker House Publishers).

42 Written on a business card that Leonard Ravenhill used to have. Steve Hill spoke of this in a sermon preached during the Brownsville Revival called, "Legacy."

43 Benny Hinn, "The Purpose of Pentecost," audio message.

44 From the interview with Heidi Baker in the movie, *Finger of God*.

[45] David Hogan, *Faith to Raise the Dead* videos from Brownsville Revival School of Ministry.

[46] Madame Guyon, *Short and Easy Method of Prayer* unabridged (Public Domain).

[47] C.H. Spurgeon, *Morning and Evening* (Christian Focus Publications).

[48] John Wesley's Journal (Send the Light Publications).

[49] Benny Hinn, *This Is Your Day* television broadcast.

[50] A.W. Tozer, *The Pursuit of God* (Christian Publications, Inc.).

[51] Charles Spurgeon, *Morning and Evening* (Christian Focus Publications).

[52] Dr. Michael L. Brown, *Spiritual Hunger* audio sermon from the Brownsville Revival.

[53] Charles Finney, *Power from on High*, Innocent Amusements chapter (Whitaker House Publishers).

[54] Art Katz, audio sermon *Sonship*.

[55] Hudson Taylor, *One With Christ* (Whitaker Publications).

[56] Dr. Michael L. Brown, *Called to Die* audio sermon from the Brownsville Revival.

[57] Leonard Ravenhill.

[58] Wigglesworth Standard (Whitaker House).

[59] John G. Lake, Kenneth Copeland Ministries.

[60] This is taken from E.M. Bounds' *E.M. Bounds on Prayer* quoting C.H. Spurgeon.

[61] I think this man was Praying Payson of Portland.

[62] E.M. Bounds, *E.M. Bounds on Prayer*.

[63] E.M. Bounds, *E.M. Bounds on Prayer*.

[64] E.M. Bounds, *E.M. Bounds on Prayer*.

[65] Leonard Ravenhill, *Why Revival Tarries* (Bethany House Publications).

[66] Steve Hill, *On Earth As It Is In Heaven* (Together in the Harvest Ministries).

[67] This is a random connection of some of my favorite quotes from the compilations, *Selah II, Prayer*, and *Selah*. www.agonypress.org

[68] Dr. Michael L. Brown, *Called to Die* message from Brownsville Assembly of God, 1999.

[69] Leonard Ravenhill on Tozer, audio compilation, *We Won't All Be the Same in Heaven*. www.agonypress.org

[70] I heard Leonard Ravenhill say this in a sermon years back. It hit me so hard I never forgot it. I cannot recall the sermon title.

[71] Jeremy Taylor, *Holy Living* (Paraclete Press).

[72] This is the slogan of the Sisters of Mary.

[73] Quoted in Samuel Chadwick's *The Path of Prayer* (CLC Publications).

[74] E.M. Bounds, *Complete Works of E.M. Bounds.*

[75] The last statement that Leonard Ravenhill made on his *A Man of God* interview.

[76] E.M. Bounds, *E.M. Bounds on Prayer.*

[77] *Webster's Dictionary.*

[78] This is a short compiling of some of my favorite quotes by Bill Johnson, from audio sermons from the Bethel podcast.

[79] An article I read online called "Livingness" by T. Austin Sparks (All of T. Austin Sparks' writings are free).

[80] Steve Hill, Together in the Harvest, is the one that I heard say this.

[81] David Popovici, FIRE school Chicago.

[82] Reinhard Bonnke, "Woman at the Well" sermon preached at Calvary Assembly, Winter Park, Florida.

[83] K.P. Yohannan, "Christ's Call to Follow His Footsteps" audio message.

[84] Bill Johnson, *Heaven on Earth* compilation from www.agonypress.org.

85 An issue of *Charisma* magazine that was geared toward evangelism, compiled by Reinhard Bonnke and Daniel Kolenda.

86 Bill Johnson, *When Heaven Invades Earth* (Destiny Image Publishers).

87 YouTube interview on healing with Bill Johnson.

88 Art Katz, audio sermon from sermonindex.com.

89 F.B. Meyer (Quoted in Andrew Murray's book, *The State of the Church, An Urgent Call to Repentance and Prayer*, page 41).

90 I heard him say this in the 8 a.m. to 10 a.m. daily prayer meeting at FIRE in 2001.

91 Pastor Andrew Lamb, Acts 2 Church in Longwood, Florida.

92 Art Katz, "To God Be the Glory in the Church" audio sermon from sermonindex.com.

93 *Life Together* (Fortress Press).

94 *"Apostolic Community"* audio from FIRE school of ministry by Dr. Robert Gladstone.

95 Travis Fisher, a friend of mine, told me this.

96 Gregory Boyd from the movie, *Furious Love*.

97 John G. Lake, *Complete Life Teachings*, Roberts Liardon (Albury Publications).

[98] Healing sermon by Bill Johnson, Bethel.

[99] A few tremendous healing books to read further on such a subject are *Healing the Sick* by T.L. Osborn and *Christ Our Healer* by F.F. Bosworth.

Made in the USA
Lexington, KY
19 November 2019